For the Love of Oceans

Atlantic and Eastern Caribbean Islands
Baltimore, MD to Saint Thomas USVI

J. Hubbard Pink

Printed in the United States of America

First Printing December 2022

ISBN 978-1-956661-36-1 Paperback

ISBN 978-1-956661-37-8 Hardcover

Published by: Book Services
www.BookServices.us

Dedication

To my mom, Marianne A. Hubbard (1927-2020)

She was an amazing human being and an endless source of unconditonal love and encouragement.

Acknowledgments

I owe the deepest gratitude to my patient, loving, and kind husband. My writing has taken me back to a time before him as I relived my ocean adventures. I would read to him as I wrote. He would listen, laugh with me, sometimes shake his head, but always give me a loving smile.

Thank you to my three children. Although they were independent at the time of my adventures, they were impacted by my taking an uncommon, and to most people, a daring journey in my new empty-nest reality.

Thank you to Jack and Cap and to all the people I met on this journey. Each of them makes the story complete.

And thank you to my editor, Betsy, who looked at a book I had started and shelved over ten years ago because I was not happy with it. Her excitement for me to tell the story of my travels and her encouragement for me to tell that story in my own words was immeasurable.

Contents

Foreword

Was the ocean calling me? From childhood, I had a deep love and respect for the ocean. Then, suddenly, I was a widow. What do you do when life doesn't go as planned? You can lock yourself away in a closet, or you can open your eyes and ears to possibilities. So, when an unexpected opportunity arose to crew for my friend Jack, I made the choice to see parts of the globe from a unique and different perspective, to experience it in a way that I had never imagined in my wildest dreams. My passion for the ocean and the underwater world, only grew stronger after my months along the coast of Central America, so I soon looked for another job crewing on a sailboat, this time making the trip from Baltimore, Maryland to Margarita Island, Venezuela. This volume covers the segment from Baltimore to the Virgin Islands.

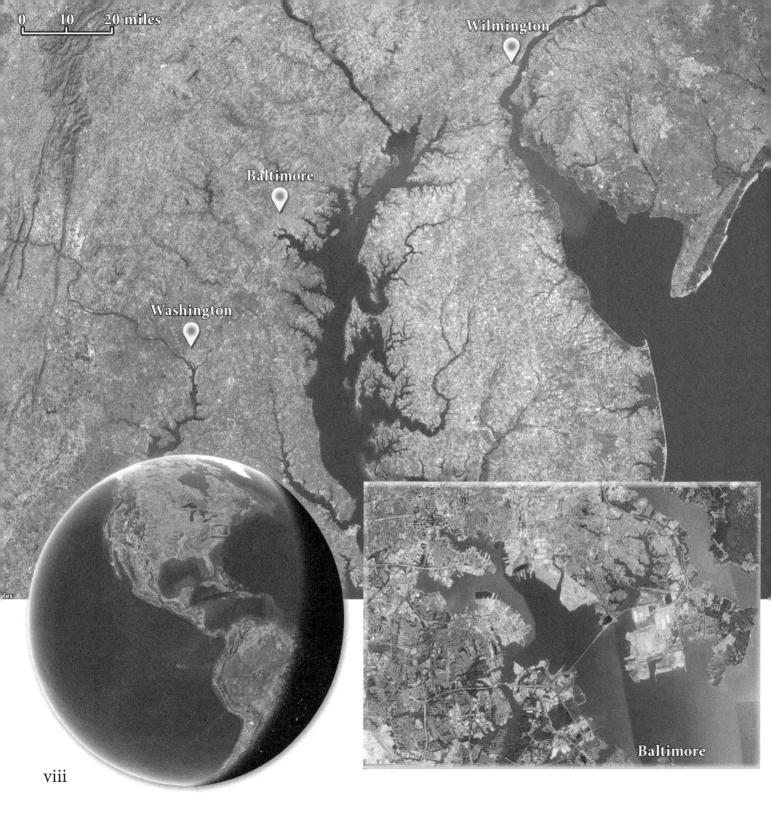

0   10   20 miles

Wilmington

Baltimore

Washington

iles

viii

Baltimore

Chapter 1

A Different Sailboat, Baltimore, Maryland

After my adventures crewing from Zihuantanejo, Mexico to Costa Rica for my friend Jack, my land sickness—my temporary inability to walk on solid ground like a landlubber without looking drunk—had subsided, but my desire to be back out on the ocean was stronger than ever. I was back in Washington State, where I spent the summer of 2007 looking for a sailboat. I looked at a few and got fairly serious about one in a marina in Bellingham. I felt I was a capable sailor after my months on Jack's 36-foot C & C. I knew, however, that I did not want to sail alone. I began looking for crew so I would be prepared when I found a sailboat that clicked all the boxes for me. I found a promising website. Unfortunately, I found nothing I would be able to afford if I were to buy a boat and pay all of its maintenance and expenses. I put my sailboat purchase on hold.

However, on the same website I found people looking for crew. As I scrolled through the ads, one in particular caught my eye: a kind-looking disabled gentleman with a sailboat looking for crew. I began a dialogue with him. Cap and his wife had worked their entire lives with the goal of buying a sailboat and sailing the Caribbean when he retired. Sadly, his wife passed away before the boat was delivered. Cap and his 53-foot Amel Super Maramou sailboat, the *Lady*, were in a marina in Baltimore, Maryland.

I had never been to Baltimore. I'd never even had the suspicion of a desire to go.

In September, I flew to Baltimore to meet Cap and his friends and to learn more about his sailboat and his sailing plans. He was as kind as he had appeared in his picture. Earlier in the year he'd had knee surgery for a second time. And a year or two before that he'd had a few back surgeries. He needed crew to help do the jobs on the boat that he no longer could because of his physical limitations. He used a cane and was very slow getting around. Plus, his carrying weight limit was perhaps one grocery bag filled with lightweight groceries.

Cap was passionate about his sailboat from ◆bow to ◆stern. He knew how every system worked, and he spent endless hours researching the Internet for better (and less expensive) spare parts, tirelessly making sure ◆"she" (*Lady*) was working at 100 percent plus. He had installed a fuel-polishing system of which he was very proud, believing that most issues with diesel engines come from bad fuel. He believed that as long as the engine got clean fuel, it would run. How he loved *Lady*! And she was a beautiful boat: a 53-foot ◆center cockpit ◆ketch.

Lady was basically, as Cap would say, an all-electric sailboat. There was a diesel generator to keep the batteries charged up when needed. Both the ◆mainsail and ◆mizzen sail had in-mast furling with the switches to furl and unfurl inside the cockpit on the ◆cockpit dash. All the winches used to tighten the sails were electric. Inside the cockpit on the dash were gauges that showed the strength of the winds and the best point of sail with the existing wind. The stern had a ◆sugar scoop transom that helped Cap get on and off the boat in the marina when positioned stern to dock, but also helped him get into the dinghy when anchored out. There was no need for a ladder over the side. What a difference from Jack's sailboat! I was in awe!

Going down below through the ◆companionway hatch I found the galley directly to port (on the left) and a navigation ("nav") station to starboard (on the right). The nav station could be seen from the cockpit by looking down the companionway hatch. The galley had a gimbled gas stovetop and stove. The sink was much like the sink in the galley on Jack's 36-foot C&C sailboat, just larger. And larger wasn't the only difference. Much like a house faucet, the handle only had to be turned with the pump switch on to get water into the sink because there was an electric pump, not a manual foot pump. There was a ◆reverse osmosis desalination watermaker. Cap's boat could make water! And there was a small stand-up fridge, a microwave, a clothes washer, *and* a dishwasher. Yes, a real electric dishwasher that was not *me*!

The salon had a U-shaped couch to port with two chest freezers under each of the end cushions. The U-shape was around a table with a smaller couch opposite it on the starboard side. Cap told me that the small TV could get channels all the way down the coast of the United States, so he downloaded movies when he could and watched them on a computer screen.

There was a v-berth cabin in the bow and a queen cabin in the stern, both with adjoining heads. The heads were push-a-button-to-flush, so there would be no valve to remember to open or forget to close as I had in the embarrassing incident on Jack's boat. There were also showers in each head area with hot running water. No more showering with sun-warmed water in my swimsuit in the cockpit! And finally, there were three heating/air conditioning units, one for each section of the boat and a lot of batteries onboard under a gangway/hallway bunk. This sailboat seemed to have everything!

Cap's friends at the marina were warm and welcoming. The marina manager, Bill, was a one-in-a-million kind of guy. Cap was friends with two other couples in the marina, and when I met them, they embraced me as a fellow cruiser.

The Annapolis boat show was the following week. We made plans to make the short sail from Baltimore to Annapolis and attend for a day.

I was so amazed at the sailing difference between Cap's boat and Jack's boat. The *Lady* was bigger, longer, and wider; she sailed so smooth and fast compared to Jack's boat. *Lady's* hull speed was up to 10 knots (11 ½ mph). Cap liked going fast. He said that his boat liked 35 knots of wind, since it could then sail at a hull speed of 10 knots, sometimes more. He downloaded ◆GRIB files (wind and wave files that are superimposed on the chart plotter) onto his computer to show wind and wave height. He also had a computer dedicated to the chart plotter, which had maps of the East Coast and the Caribbean. No need for manual plotting on this sailboat. The autopilot would keep us on our entered route while sailing or motoring even if there was current! He explained that all it took was one connecting wire to establish communication between the GPS and the autopilot. It was like coming out of the 19th century (Jack's sailboat) into the 21st century—maybe a bit of an exaggeration, but it would be a whole new way of learning to sail. I watched Cap handle the sailboat, motoring, sailing, and anchoring all from the captain's chair in the cockpit. I was excited and ready to watch and learn.

The number of boats of all kinds in Annapolis was stunning. We anchored in the bay and took the dinghy off of the deck space aft of the cockpit via the mizzen halyard. Cap wound the line onto the winch and slowly released it so the dinghy would gently splash down into the water. Then he took the halyard and attached it to the engine. He got into the dinghy and I lowered the engine down gently until it was positioned perfectly. He hooked up the fuel tank to the engine and off we went in to the dinghy dock, locking our dinghy securely. It was great fun to tour all the different sailboats and trawlers with salesmen aboard and to look at all the exhibits. Cap was intrigued by an anchor exhibit, and I bought a few fishing lures.

Putting the engine and dinghy back up on the deck was fairly easy with the electric winch. Once it was secured to the back deck over the aft cabin, we lifted anchor, which was made easier by the anchor windlass. Neither Cap nor I had to manually pull the anchor ◆rode back into the boat! Back to Baltimore and the marina we motor-sailed.

Cap and I decided that we would begin a trip south in early November, going down the East Coast to Florida, over to the Bahamas, and down to Isla Margarita off the coast of Venezuela, returning to Baltimore sometime in the spring. I would pay for all the food and provisions and any diving costs; he would maintain the sailboat and pay for fuel. We would split any side travels. Cap knew I was passionate about being under the ocean. He looked at that as an opportunity to get the bottom of his sailboat cleaned without having to haul it out of the water. We would leave Baltimore after I returned from a trip to Zihuantanejo that I had previously planned with a girlfriend.

The *Lady* was only three years old, yet there seemed to be a lot of maintenance expenses. Cap grumbled about the costs, but he did what was needed to keep her in great sailing condition. During the summer he had purchased a new mainsail ($2,800), had a radar repair ($1,150), a generator repair ($1,100), a new anchor shackle ($321), and new ◆jenny sheets ($174). He was still doing research on the best anchor, knowing that it would cost just under $1,000, and he was having voltage regulator issues. He was happpy to find out he could have the voltage regulator replaced under warranty.

I flew back to Baltimore after my Zihuantanejo (Z) to Seattle road trip on October 24th. I had decided to bring the car that my mom and I had taken down to Z (See *For the Love of Oceans, Zihuantanejo to Costa Rica*) back to Washington. I somehow knew that living in Z was not something I wanted to do again. Looking at and listening to the ocean from the shore would not be enough for me now. My girlfriend and I had a great time driving through Mexico and California, staying at hotels and shopping, but I was anxious to get back to the *Lady* and Cap. The draw of the ocean was too strong. I was ready to begin a new adventure.

While I was gone, Cap had been going to physical therapy three times a week. He was walking better, but still in quite a bit of pain. We began provisioning the sailboat for our trip south. It involved a lot of shopping, and shopping for the best deals was something that Cap thoroughly enjoyed. We borrowed a car from one of Cap's friends and filled the old station wagon seven or eight times with groceries and dry goods. Cap and I were having so much fun provisioning the boat that he was actually waiting patiently (for him) for the generator to be repaired. On one of our provisioning runs I made sure to buy some postcards and send them to my mom and my children.

Lucky for me, Cap was passionate about food and cooking. He loved to eat. Thankfully, he also loved to cook, as my cooking was nowhere near as good as his. I cooked a breakfast or two a week between cereal breakfasts, and Cap cooked huge, wonderful dinners with lots of leftovers. All I needed to do was to clean the galley once he was done cooking and we were done eating. Cleaning the galley, however, was no easy chore, as Cap could make quite a mess. I told Cap that he should write a cookbook and a Caribbean provisioning book. His meals were really that spectacular.

Baltimore

Chapter 1 - A Different Sailboat, Baltimore, Maryland

As we carted everything from the car down the marina piers to the boat, we joked that we were lowering the water line. Which indeed, we probably did a little. Cap's boat could store a lot of goods.

They say timing is everything. The generator was repaired on Friday and on Saturday, November 2, 2007 we sailed out of Baltimore after saying our final goodbyes and thank-yous to all at the Inner Harbor East Marina.

Baltimore

Washington

Solomons Island

Deltaville

Norfolk

Hatteras

0   25   50 miles

Chapter 2

Down the Chesapeake to Norfolk, Virginia

We motored out of the harbor and turned south. We had a great wind of 15 to 20 knots. Cap unfurled the sails by pressing different switches on the cockpit dash and turned off the engine. I watched in awe. The *Lady* was fantastically smooth in the 8-plus knots of wind. Using the switches on the cockpit dash, Cap also deftly adjusted the sails continually in order to trim them to get the best sailboat knot speed relative to the knots of wind.

About three hours into our sail, Cap asked me to release some of the jenny sheet from the winch. No problem,

I thought. I had done that many times on Jack's sailboat. I either let it go too fast or wasn't ready for the wind to yank it so hard. Probably both. The wind took the whole starboard line out and away from me and the winch! It wrapped the line around and around the jenny so fast that nothing Cap did from the helm with the cockpit switches would release and untangle the line. Three hours into our sail and I had really screwed up. I went down below and started crying.

Cap started the engine. I couldn't stay crying long, as Cap called for my help topside to try to untangle the mess. I wiped by tears away and jumped into the cockpit. While I took the helm and steered in certain directions at his request, Cap went to the bow and took on the job, first trying to manually untangle the line and when that wasn't happening, he started cutting the old line. It took 45 minutes of cutting in a lot of places with me sometimes steering in circles to get the jenny sheets untangled, albeit the starboard side was in pieces.

Luckily, Cap had already purchased new jenny sheets. We had talked about replacing them before we left because they were frayed in places, but it was one of the chores that we hadn't gotten to yet. Also luckily, only one side was in pieces, and we could still sail with the jenny. That was a slight relief. We chatted about what had happened. I had only wrapped the line on the winch twice around before cleating it off. That was all that was ever needed with Jack's boat and the winds we had on the Pacific Coast. We decided that wrapping three times would be the best way to prevent the wind from taking control of the jenny sheet again with the bigger boat and bigger sails. Cap was so wonderful not to be upset with me.

The wind started and stopped a few times in the afternoon. With the help of the new mainsail shape and in spite of the jenny sheet delay, we were able to make it to Solomons Island, Maryland and anchor just before dark. The most difficult part of anchoring with Cap's sailboat was knowing where to anchor and what ◆scope of chain (how much extra chain) to put out. What most call ideal is a 7:1 ratio, i.e., 7 feet of rode (in our case chain) for every foot of water depth. Cap liked between 7:1 and 10:1 for his anchoring safety. He also showed me how to put on what he called a ◆snubber.

Solomons Island

The good news was that we had plenty of snubber material from the jenny line that had been cut. Both letting out the anchor and bringing the anchor in was done with a switch inside the cockpit. I was feeling pretty lucky in this beautiful spot. So many boats to look at...so little time.

Anchored in the Solomons

Cove Point Lighthouse

Deltaville

Solomons Lump Lighthouse

Cap had sailed up and down the East Coast many times and had already tentatively planned our trip to Key West, Florida. He wanted to show me his favorite little towns along the way. We were in a sailboat, however, and he preferred to sail, rather than to motor sail, which meant that our town stops and timing would be wind dependent.

We motor-sailed to Deltaville, Virginia the next morning and dropped anchor late in the afternoon. Then the wind quit.

Deltaville

Calm winds in Deltaville

The next morning there was still no wind. It was completely calm. It was warm and sunny, however, so it became a day for chores.

Cap started the generator to recharge the batteries. It ran for only a few minutes and then quit. It had just been fixed before we left Baltimore by service technicians. Cap was able to narrow the diagnosis to the newly replaced switch. Thankfully, he had two spares. As he was disconnecting the old one, he saw that there was a loose ground which had probably burned out the contactor. He fixed the ground, put in a spare switch, and the generator ran smoothly.

The situation reminded me of when I was sitting with the ladies at the Barillas Marina in El Salvador, listening to the guys with all their ideas about sailboat fixes. Cap was a diagnose-and- fix-it himself kind of guy. Perhaps his attitude was just a necessary part of the sailboat culture. There is not always a repair person to call.

All the chores we wanted to accomplish were dependent on electrical power, i.e., the generator. Once that was repaired, Cap cleaned the watermaker membrane with a cleaner meant for restoring it to a good, usable condition. The water in the bucket was an ugly brown, so I was very happy to see it cleaned. He put the membranes back into the watermaker, turned it on, and flushed the first bit of water overboard before we began to fill the tank.

Deltaville sunset

Cap showed me how to start the clothes washer. He then directed me as I pulled a propeller knotmeter out of the hull of the boat from inside the boat and pushed a cork-type plug in so the salt water would not flow in. The knotmeter looked like it hadn't been cleanerd since Cap bought the sailboat, so I cleaned it in the sink before quickly removing the plug and returning it back to the hole in the hull. I was working in a very cramped space, and I needed to be quick to keep water from flowing into the boat. I felt pretty accomplished about completing that chore with minimal Chesapeake Bay water coming into the hull.

We replaced the old nylon jenny sheets with the new ones. That felt good too. After the clothes washer had completed its spin cycle and shut off, I took the clothes into the cockpit. I secured a clothesline around three or four ◆shrouds, then hung and clipped (in case the wind did begin to blow) the wet clothes up to dry in the sun. Yes, there was a clothes dryer: the sun and the wind.

The next day we sailed down the Chesapeake Bay to Norfolk, Virginia with only a few hours of it motor sailing. It was a cold sail. I mainly stayed down below out of the wind. I remarked to Cap how cold the toilet seats were. I didn't remember the toilet seats being cold on Jack's boat. That became Cap's goal: to get us far enough south that the toilet seats were warm. For me it was about diving too. I really wanted to go diving. Of course, I had my dive gear with me.

There were a lot of sailboats behind us, almost like they were following us. Those boats headed south would probably take "the ditch," as Cap called it, slang for the ◆Intracoastal Waterway (ICW). Cap's sailboat was too tall. The mast was 66' tall, too tall to go under most of the bridges. It was also too deep. *Lady's* ◆winged keel was 7' below the hull, too deep for some of the ICW shallow waters. We would have to go on what Cap called the "outside,"—around Cape Hatteras and off the coast. It would be a double overnight passage.

He rolled all the sails and started the engine as we got to the mouth of the Elizabeth River. We motored by the military vessels in Norfolk and anchored off the Naval Hospital near the start of the ditch (ICW) or as some say "mile zero." Cap then made a wonderful garlic rosemary lamb cooked in wine with tomatoes over pasta. I didn't know when I had ever eaten so well. And on a sailboat!

We were following the weather closely, looking for a good weather window to go around Hatteras. It looked like we would have good wind for sailing around Hatteras in a couple of days, so Cap decided to fuel up before we left Norfolk just in case the weather changed. It was cold, and I was really looking forward to getting farther south and into warmer weather.

Helicopter towing in a training target

Military parachute exercises

Passing military vessel

Norfolk Virginia

Cape Henry Lighthouse

Norfolk Virginia

After we fueled up, we motored out to a safe anchorage that Cap knew about. It was close to the Atlantic, so we could get an early start on our passage the next day. We passed the three-masted ship, the *Statsraad Lehmkuhl*, an 84-foot three-masted barque-rigged training vessel out of Norway, as it motored into Norfolk. What a beautiful ship! She made the *Lady* seem so small. I would have loved to see her under sail, but I was also so very glad I was not doing chores on her. Once re-anchored, we did two loads of laundry and watched the Navy play with their helicopters and little boats. After the laundry had dried, we put up *Lady's* ◆down-wind pole system.

0 50 100 miles

Norfolk

Cape Hatteras

Morehead City

Wrightsville Beach

Charleston

Fernandina Beach

Chapter 3
Back-to-back Storms

I didn't know much about Cape Hatteras, North Carolina. Cap told me there were more shipwrecks off this coast than in any other region. I wasn't sure if that was true, but since he brought it up, I looked up the area on my computer. I found that over the centuries Cape Hatteras has been called a deadly trap for sailors. This stretch of shore is the final resting place of more than 600 shipwrecks off the shifting sandbars of the Hatteras Islands. The depth is relatively shallow (50 to 60 feet), and the sandbars shift due to the rough waves and unpredictable currents. After reading about the shipwrecks, I grew nervous and a bit jealous of the "ditch diggers," as Cap so fondly called them. They could miss this treacherous part of the coast by taking the ICW.

Cap was pretty sure from his downloaded GRIB files that we would have a good window for the next two days to get around Cape Hatteras. The wind would be from the right direction. It wouldn't be too strong, but enough to sail. He expected we'd have some motor-sailing to get to the turn at Cape Hatteras, but once we made the turn, it would be great wind sailing. I guess I should mention that I didn't check on Cap's GRIB files. He would talk to me about them as he looked at them, and we would talk about where we were going, but I never actually looked at them or questioned him. Our plan was to bypass Beaufort, North Carolina and go right on to Wrightsville Beach. It would be a double overnight, but we'd be making southerly gains towards warmer weather.

We left the next morning with the expected wind coming from behind. It was still cold. Cap plugged an electric heater into a step-down transformer to keep the salon warm. At one point we were going 7.6 knots in 15.4 knots of wind. We had the generator running, and we were making water. It was 70 degrees in the salon, and we were watching TV, all while keeping an eye on the radar. Was this really okay? I was thinking about my time on Jack's sailboat. Was *this* cold weather sailing? I will admit I was loving it and feeling just a bit spoiled.

The wind didn't last; it wasn't strong enough to fill the sails with the down-wind pole system, so we ended up motoring the rest of the day, following the ◆ten-fathom curve (60 feet) about five miles off the coast.

I took the first shift, 9:00 p.m. to midnight. There was no manual charting to worry about, so I bundled up in the cockpit, watched for lights, watched the radar, and watched *Lady's* course. Being the first overnight on this sailboat and being on watch all alone was nerve-racking. The *Lady* had a larger cockpit to pace, and the time passed slowly. For days, I had watched and listened to Cap talk about his beloved sailboat, and I certainly did not want to miss anything that could cause an issue. Just before I woke Cap up for his shift, there was a one-of-a-kind shooting star: blue-green with a yellow and red tail. It lasted a very long time, though not long enough for a picture.

Cap woke me up around four in the morning when we were about to make the turn so I could see the infamous Cape Hatteras light. I tried to take a picture of the light…in the dark…don't look for that picture anytime soon.

The turn was about a mile east of the light. As soon as we made the turn, the wind jumped to 20 to 30 knots. Wow! Glad that was not before the turn. Cap adjusted the sails, and we were able to turn the engine off and sail. We checked the ◆VHF weather. There was no mention of 30-plus gusts. Oh well, this is what we had. The seas were confused, the gusts over 30 knots, and we were sailing on a ◆beam reach on our way to Wrightsville Beach.

As Cap had been telling me, the *Lady* really did enjoy 20-plus knots. However, gusts of over 30 knots were another story. It would have been more fun if it had been daylight. Of course, daylight came, and the wind continued. The waves were pretty steep by that time, so the *Lady's* bow was lurching skyward, then pounding down with the water washing over the bow. That pretty much summed up our day: strong winds, ◆heeling, bow up and down. We decided that quick sandwiches was all I was going to make for lunch and dinner, as the sailboat movement made being down

below a bit more challenging. I rather relished the challenge, at least long enough to make the sandwiches. Truth be told, I felt a surge of joy because I had finally gotten my sea legs back. And that felt really good.

Cap had the sails trimmed so that we were moving at 8.6 knots in 36.9 knots of wind. The sun came out and the temperature got to almost 62, still too cold for my taste, but what a sail! If we kept up sailing at this speed, we would get into Wrightsville Beach at two in the morning however, so Cap brought the sails in to slow the *Lady* down.

Just past Morehead City we made another turn towards Wrightsville Beach and then the wind quit. Cap had to start the engine to motor sail along at 5 knots. He was feeling a

lot of pain in his back from the extreme boat movement of the last few days. Luckily, he had prescription medicine that helped. We were both looking forward to getting off the boat and doing a bit of walking.

I fell asleep in the late afternoon. When Cap woke me up for my night watch, he mentioned that the radar seemed to be having issues; it was not seeing things like buoys and other boats so he warned me to be sure to keep a sharp lookout.

There was another shooting star. I was enjoying this night watch, even given the extra task of watching through the binoculars, until the GPS started giving the error message: OFF COURSE. I waited a little while; then I got worried. When I was going down the Pacific with Jack and the GPS was off, I didn't panic too much because I was keeping manual charts. But what if I really *was* off course. In the dark it is a little hard to tell, and I forgot to get the ◆course in degrees on the compass before Cap went to sleep. I woke him up after only two hours of sleep. He got us going on a better course anyway—sailing, rather than beating into the wind, so all was good, except for his loss of sleep.

After sleeping another couple of hours, Cap took over the helm, and I went back to bed. I woke up when I was suddenly tossed to the other side of the bed. Cap had ◆tacked! We were still sailing, but now pounding through the waves in 30 to 38 knot winds into Wrightsville Beach, North Carolina.

Getting close, Cap rolled up the sails, turned on the engine, and we motored into the Masonboro Inlet. Once quietly in anchorage, we did some laundry and the dishes. We took the dinghy off of the deck space aft of the cockpit via the mizzen halyard and then lowered the engine too. It was a 15 horsepower pull-to-start engine, and I noticed that it was difficult for Cap to pull more than a few times to get it started. I told him that if it didn't start on the second pull, I should pull from my angle. That seemed to work great.

Wrightsville Beach

We motored over to a dinghy dock and went into the town. It was a cute beach town, but pretty much deserted. Everyone else must be thinking it was too cold as well and had already headed south. The ICW (Intercoastal Waterway) connects here. I walked over to the local post office, bought some postcards, and sent them to my mom and the kids.

The next morning, Cap called the radar manufacturer. He'd had an issue with his autopilot the previous year. It was made by the same manufacturer, so he had all the names and numbers of people to call. A technician called him back and walked him through setting up the radar. Cap had picked up the sailboat brand new, yet no one had ever set up the radar or told him how to set it up himself. Following the technician's instructions, Cap got the radar working better than ever, and we could see the position of every boat in the harbor. It was such a relief to know that we would not need to use the binoculars as much as we had on the last passage.

We took the dinghy over to the restaurant at the Dockside Marina right next to the ICW. Cap ordered a softshell crab sandwich for each of us. It was touted as an East Coast delicacy. Being from the West Coast, I had never had one. It was to be eaten shell and all. Now, I loved what I considered to be *real* crab, Dungeness Crab. I had no problem spending the hours it took to clean every piece of the meat out of the shell to

Wrightsville Beach

Dockside Marina

eat it. But eating the shell of a crab? I was skeptical. The crab was battered and deep-fried and served on a bun with lettuce and sauce. I started out slowly, eating only a few of the legs. Then I ate more of the battered crab. In fact, I ended up eating *all* of the battered crab! To my surprise, it was delicious.

From the restaurant we watched the boats as they motored south through the ICW. At noon they opened a bridge to let a pack of the ditch diggers through. Wow! Listen to *me*. I'm sounding like Cap. I was indulging in a little bit of verbal chest-pounding for having sailed on the "outside," around Cape Hatteras. A four-masted cruise ship motored by with all four masts cut off—shortened so it could go under all the 65-foot bridges on the ICW.

Friends from the marina in Baltimore had left three weeks ahead of us. Cap called them and found they were in Charleston, South Carolina, our next stop. Going down the ICW, boats can only make 50 or 60 miles a day. We had sailed and motored 275 miles in three days. We opted for a day of rest, but there was no wind anyway, so our plan was to head to Charleston the next day. With west winds at 10 to 15 knots, it should be a nice calm sail. It would be an overnight of 30 hours or so to make the 100 miles to Charleston. We talked about doing a little re-provisioning in Charleston before continuing south.

Sailing on the "outside," around Cape Hatteras

Chapter 3 - Back-to-back storms

We left Wrightsville Beach around 10:30 in the morning after securing the dinghy onto the back deck of the *Lady*. The forecast was for a light wind from the west with southwest winds coming later in the passage, hopefully after rounding Cape Fear, North Carolina.

 Once on the outside, we were able to motor sail for about an hour. The southwest winds started sooner than forecast and put the 8 knots of wind directly on our nose! We furled the sails and increased the engine rpm's.

There was only a sliver of a moon over the bow on my watch. It seemed to be the largest sliver of a moon that I had ever seen. Of course, there is no picture of that. You'll have to trust me.

I have to admit that I got a little mixed up a few times as we headed south down the coast. The land was on the starboard side, with sunsets over land and sunrises over the ocean. I grew up on the West Coast, where sunrises were over land and sunsets over water when you were out in a boat. Of course, that was also true during the months I crewed for Jack—sunsets were always over the ocean. It was a very good thing that the *Lady* had an autopilot or there is no telling where we might have gone in the dark. Before this passage where I was on night watch, I made sure to get the course in degrees from Cap since we were not charting manually. That way, if I got too worried I could just check the compass.

We continued to motor and burn fuel on Cap's watch as the winds continued to blow too lightly and straight into the bow. Once we rounded Cape Fear, Cap turned the engine off and we were able to sail. From Cap's perspective, it was a very slow sail. In 9 to 11 knots of wind the *Lady* was going 4.8 to 5.4 knots. But we were sailing, not motoring. When I was on Jack's sailboat I had considered 4 to 5 knots a great sail.

The next day we started seeing lots of birds: pelicans, seagulls, and various other seabirds. Many dolphins swam alongside us on this passage, and I even saw a little turtle. Cap showed me how he talked to the dolphins in his made-up dolphin language, and he swore that they understood him. No, I did not think he was crazy. I talked to the Pacific coast dolphins in my travels with Jack. And everyone who knows me, knows that when I was living in Zihuantanejo, Mexico, I talked to the geckos in my condo in English, sure that they understood me!

I was getting anxious to go diving, to immerse myself in the ocean. I expected that the first opportunity to do so would be in Florida. Cap had mentioned that the bottom of the hull needed to be scraped. That would be my chore. My only request was that we be anchored in clear waters so I would at least be able to look around a little while breathing underwater.

We passed the Sullivan Island lighthouse and entered the channel to Charleston, South Carolina about 4:30 in the afternoon. The temperature finally in the 70s, and the sun on my skin felt wonderful. I might be able to put my winter hat, gloves, wool socks, and three layers of clothes away soon.

One of the many perks of cruising is seeing spectacular works of nature's art, sunrises and sunsets, right from the cockpit of the boat. Another perk is being rocked to sleep by the waves, with the only sound being the water lightly touching the hull. Then there were days when we were anchored, and there was no movement and no sound. That was what I woke up to the morning after we anchored in Charleston. Well that, and once I was awake, the shrimp making their crackling noise, something I had not heard since sailing down the Pacific coast.

From where we were anchored, we could see Charleston's stunning new bridge. Cap started listening to weather first thing in the morning and downloading GRIB weather files. We had two options as he saw it. Wait another day and rest

Charleston

up, but then have only 5 to 20 knots of wind out of the northwest for sailing on an overnight to Fernandina Beach or St. Augustine, Florida. (I already knew that was not really an option; he was just being nice.) Or we could leave today and sail with southwest winds at 15 to 20 knots, changing to west around one o'clock, then northwest by four in the afternoon with 20 to 30 knots staying less than 20 miles offshore. Of course, there really was only one option, and the decision was made to go today. I hurriedly got the boat secured for our sail. We left about 10:30 in the morning and motored out into the incoming tide past Fort Sumter and out to sea. By eleven we were sailing, with Cap having to trim the sails as close to the wind as possible—a technique called ◆pinching—as our desired course was almost directly into the wind.

He set our course onto what he called vane, i.e. a wind vane. Sailing on a wind vane is a technique in which the sails are set to a specific wind angle to the boat. The course of the boat then changes based on the direction of the wind to the sails. We were sailing comfortably at 7 to 8 knots, expecting to stay

Fort Sumter

close to shore, based on the forecast of the wind changing direction at one o'clock. We turned up the radio and were enjoying the sunny day and the sail. The seas were even comfortable, as we were off a lee shore. This meant that the wind was blowing off the beach, and the waves were much smaller since they did not have time and distance to build up.

We were so enjoying the day and the sail that it was well after two when we noticed that the wind was increasing along with the wave height. The wind had shifted, and our course had been changing slightly for hours. That meant we had gone much farther offshore than planned.

The winds increased into the 20s, then into 30-plus knots. The seas had grown quickly to the four to six-foot range and were more confused because the wind direction was different from the existing wave pattern. Cap continued to reef the main and the jenny sail as the wind velocity increased. After the winds we had experienced around Cape Hatteras, Cap had changed one of the readouts on his cockpit dash to the ◆Beaufort scale. It was currently reading F 6, which is considered a strong breeze, with wind speeds to 27 knots and a probable wave height of 9 to 10 feet. Then it went to a steady F 7, considered a near gale or moderate gale with wind speeds to 33 knots and probable wave height of 13 to 14 feet. One of the footnotes under the Beaufort F 7 readout was that yachts were to remain in harbor and those at sea to ◆lie to.

The gale was really quite fun for a while. It was giving me increasing confidence in what the *Lady* could handle and what I myself could handle. I was taking pictures and video and getting the salt spray in my face as the *Lady* pounded into the waves at 7 knots. It was a fantastic, exhilarating ride.

It also gave me confidence in Cap's handling of the sails and the sailboat. When the winds got to gale force, F 8, with wind speeds up to 40 knots, probable wave height of 18 feet, and a footnote stating that all yachts should make for harbor if possible, Cap furled in the main sail completely, let a hanky of the mizzen out, left a hanky of the jenny out, and we sailed ◆gin and jigger. We were still moving along at 6 to 7 knots.

By evening the hours and hours of high wind with high breaking waves, the gale started to get old and cold. The winds reached F 9. On the Beaufort scale, that registered as a strong gale with wind speeds to 47 knots and probable wave heights of 23 feet. Waves were breaking over the ◆foredeck with a wave every once in a while slapping us ◆amidships and 20 to 30 gallons of water crashing over the ◆hard dodger. Cap was very happy he had ordered the *Lady* with the hard dodger. The volume of water coming over the top of the decks would have flattened a soft dodger. But now he started worrying about blowing out a sail.

The winds were a steady Force 9 with the seas even more confused when Cap sent me down below to start the generator and turn the salon heat on. He reefed the sails a little more and then he came below as well. He closed the cabin main hatch behind him. That was the scariest moment of the gale for me: closing the hatch while sailing underway.

There was nothing more either of us could do in the cockpit. There was a beautiful sunset and the stars were coming out, but it was not a night for star watching.

Once below with the radar on—it was working great now—we got pillows out of the cabins and piled them up on the salon settees. Lying on the salon settees with the pillows to protect us from the turbulent movement of the boat, we watched the wind instrument readout and the radar. We saw consistent winds at F 9, with a few F 10s. F 10s are designated a storm, a whole gale, with wind speeds up to 55 knots and probable wave height to 29 feet.

According to the weather forecast, the winds should be settling down by 11:30 p.m. Cap was falling asleep, so I took the first watch, which just meant that I sat in the aft settee closest to the radar and instrument readouts. When Cap relieved me about 1:30 a.m., the wind had dropped to F 7 to F 8 with gusts to F 9. I went to the aft cabin to try to sleep. At 3:30 in the morning, after maybe having slept a little bit, I relieved Cap. The winds were down to F 6 to F 7 and the *Lady* was sailing at 4 to 5 knots. Around 5:00 a.m. I went back to the aft cabin to try for more sleep. The winds were down to F 5, and the seas were down also.

At first light we went topside. When we stuck our head out the hatch, there was an unspoken, deep appreciation of the *Lady*, our safe haven. Cap put out some sail to get the *Lady* sailing back to 6 to 7 knots, and I cooked a big breakfast of eggs, along with my sprouts. It sure hit the spot, since we'd had no dinner because of the storm.

A few hours out of Fernandina Beach, Florida, a very harried and wornout little bird came onto the boat. We thought perhaps it had been through the same storm as we had and was looking for a place to relax for a little while. We arrived at Fernandina Beach, Amelia Island, about two in the afternoon. After we anchored, the bird came into the saloon. It was on the computer, on the settees, in the galley, and I was thinking to myself what a great addition it would make to the boat—except I would have bemoaned cleaning up after the mess, cleaning up after Cap *and* a bird. Thankfully, it rested up and went on its way.

We took showers and cleaned up the mess the boat had become in the gale. Everything that had not been nailed down had been tossed helter-skelter. We reviewed what had happened and what we might have done differently to avoid getting caught in such a storm. We should not have left as early as we did. We should have waited until one or two o'clock before leaving. The winds would have shifted to the west, and we would not have been pushed as far east, where the winds and seas were higher. Because we did leave early, Cap should have tacked back toward shore to keep from getting so far east and away from the shore. We were lucky. We were 25 to 30 miles offshore, and the waves were perhaps half the size that they could have been because the wind was coming from the west, and we were in the lee of the coast.

I now had the deepest regard for the *Lady*. She took care of us. And I was ever so thankful for Cap's calmness and his impressive sailing abilities.

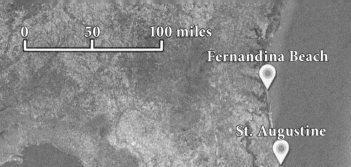

0   50   100 miles

Fernandina Beach

St. Augustine

Gulf of
Tehuantepec

Fort Pierce

West Palm Beach

Fort Lauderdale

Miami

Key West

Florida Current · Gulf Stream

Chapter 4
Florida, United States

It was our first full day anchored at Fernandina Beach, the county seat of the northernmost county on Florida's east coast. It was still colder than I liked, but at least during the day it was sunny and warm. We took the dinghy ashore for provisions and then explored the old town and Fort Clinch.

The Fort Clinch site is now a state park, with the fort itself surrounded by acres and acres of lush native flora and wildlife. The stands of live oaks draped with Spanish moss were hauntingly beautiful.

Fort Clinch itself was never completely finished because Amelia Island was deemed indefensible by the Confederates. During the Civil War, Union forces took the fort and remained in control. It was later garrisoned during the Spanish American War of 1898.

Fernandina Beach

Fort Clinch

There were shooting holes (embrasures) all around the fort. I enjoyed the ones with the view of the beach and the ocean best. On each end of the fort were parapets that gave the walls of the fort protection. Inside there was a small kitchen, a jail, a small bunkhouse area, and an ammunition storage area. And there was *one* one-hole outhouse, which was amazing, considering how many men had been stationed there.

The Amelia Island lighthouse, built in 1838, is the oldest lighthouse in Florida. It was built of materials from the former Cumberland Light-house on nearby Cumberland Island, Georgia, when that lighthouse was taken down.

Fernandina Beach is a very cute historical little town set amidst stretches of marshland. Statues stand in front of most of the downtown shops. The richness of the area's history surprised me. Amelia Island started out under French control, then Spanish control, then British control, and finally back to Spanish control with U.S. Marine protection because of piracy issues. Finally, in 1821, it was ceded to the United States and became a U.S. Territory.

Fernandina Beach

The next day we left Fernandina Beach at 7:30 a.m. with no wind and had an uneventful motor to St. Augustine, Florida. There were a lot of shrimp boats out as they like the shallow water around the inlets. It seems the shrimp go in and out with the tide. I'm not sure I could handle all the birds hanging out on and near the shrimp boats, but it was interesting to watch them.

As we approached St. Augustine, Cap radioed the Bridge of Lions and asked what their raised height was. They stated 80 feet. The *Lady* would fit under the bridge, so Cap decided to motor inside the harbor and anchor. The anchorage was crowded, but we finally found a reasonable spot and dropped anchor, although the boats were a little closer together than Cap liked.

Fernandina Beach

St. Augustine

Shrimp boat

We took the dinghy into the marina dock and walked around town the next afternoon. As usual, I bought some post-cards for my mom and kids. Writing the postcards was a fun way to share where I was with them. Like Fernandina Beach, the waterfront area was also a charming historical town. Cap's legs started to give out on him, so we stopped, had a nice lunch, and went back to the boat.

The winds had increased to 10 to 15 knots from the south with a 2 to 3 knot current in the opposite direction. It was making the *Lady* "sail" around at anchor. With all the boats so close together and each of them with different scopes out, we lifted anchor and re-anchored farther south in the anchorage. Cap wanted the *Lady* to have more room. Since we were the last boat to anchor, we were the ones who had to move, following the unwritten rules of anchorages.

That night Cap took some of his medicine and what he called his own prescription medication: a glass or two of wine. Cap did enjoy his happy-hour evenings. It seemed a lot of cruisers did. He took a cruiser test about drinking alcohol and scored a 91. I, on the other hand, was not much of a drinker, only scoring a 55; I was considered a lightweight! But Cap was adamant about not drinking on a passage until the anchor was down, for which I was very grateful!

St. Augustine

St. Augustine

We got a great deal on a rented car for a three-day weekend and decided to get some additional provisioning done. We had been eating really well, and there was now space for more frozen and dry goods. Once again, we were able to pack both freezers. Cap believed we had more food aboard than any other cruising boat around: more pickles, more green olives, more lamb, chicken, pork, corned beef, and more sausage. But with the way he cooked, we would need every bit of it. I also expected that as we got farther south into the islands, we would not be able to find some of the things we really liked, or if we did, they would be much more expensive.

I bought some fresh herbs, a pot, and some soil. I decided to try growing herbs on the boat. Fresh herbs were always wonderful, especially in my tea.

Cap called an old friend he used to work with, and we met up with him and his wife close to the marina for a drink. It was almost Thanksgiving Day. We had planned on heading south, but they invited us to their Thanksgiving Day dinner. We decided we could wait.

It was cloudy but warm in St. Augustine on Thanksgiving Day. I had started growing my sprouts after the storm, and we shared a sprout and avocado wrap for Thanksgiving Day breakfast. We checked our email and did some online catching up before taking the dinghy into the marina dock and getting picked up by Cap's friends for Thanksgiving.

We had a great time and a great meal. It was Cap's first time eating a deep-fried turkey. We both were made to feel like family. Our hosts drove us back to the marina. When we got to the dinghy, Cap couldn't find the key to unlock it. We hoped it was in the car. Cap called our friends immediately. Sure enough, they were able to find the keys, turn around, and bring them to us before we had put them out too much.

On Friday after breakfast, we readied the boat and hoisted anchor at 10:15 a.m. We were heading to Fort Pierce, 185 miles to the south. It would be another overnight. Cap started circling in front of the Bridge of Lions; there was an out-going tide of about 2 knots going under the bridge. He put the bow thruster down as a safety precaution because of the current. I asked Cap if he should radio the bridge tender to let them know of our intentions. He said no, it was not necessary.

The real Bridge of Lions was under construction. A lift bridge with a clearance of 80 feet had been built to serve the population during the two-to-three-year construction process. Cap waited as three boats went out the narrow passage and two came in. Then he squared around and started into the current-swept passage. He was watching the sides of the bridge to make sure the *Lady* was centered between the cement walls. He had us going right down the middle, motoring at around 4 knots with the current.

I was in the cockpit taking pictures of the side to show the current. When I looked up to take a picture of us going under the bridge, the bridge was coming down! I called loudly to Cap, "The bridge is coming down!" He looked up and confirmed that the bridge *was* coming down. By the time he made the confirmation, the bridge was well below the 66' mast height of the *Lady.* We were less than 50 feet from being ◆de-masted. The *Lady* was approximately 17 tons of weight going 4 knots with a 100 horsepower engine. He used more than a few expletives as he threw the boat into reverse and gave it full throttle. We were now trying to go backwards with a 2-knot current. Added to that—sailboats do not like to back up in a straight line.

I could do nothing but watch.

Cap said that two things saved the *Lady* from being demasted that day. The first was that the sailboat had an auto-prop similar to an automatic transmission. It gives the same thrust in reverse as it does in forward. When first put into gear, it takes little bites of water like a tugboat. As the boat accelerates, the prop changes shape to become more efficient at moving the boat faster. The second was that he had put the bow thruster down. He was able to steer the boat straight back with the help of the bow thruster.

He continued backing up, far enough away from the narrow passage to be able to turn around without being swept sideways into the passage by the 2-knot current. He then turned the *Lady* around and full-throttled ahead, using the bow thruster to keep the current from turning us sideways. We were motoring back into the anchorage, Cap with his heart still racing, when a Tow Boat US came alongside and asked if we were all right. Cap said yes, except for his blood pressure. The Tow Boat US guy said that Cap should call the bridge tender and then also commented, "That was some great seamanship getting out of that one."

Cap did radio the bridge tender when he had calmed down and asked why he lowered the bridge on us. The bridge tender asked if we had called in and then said he did not see us. Cap was not convinced, but there was really nothing he could do except tell him we wanted to exit on the next lifting of the bridge. I was quiet for a while, knowing there was a third thing that kept the *Lady* safe that morning. I was thinking that perhaps there was a good

reason I was aboard. I did have a lot to learn about sailing this boat, but I could be helpful now too. I was also thinking that maybe I should have just radioed the bridge tender myself. I would do that next time—if there was a next time.

Once on the outside, we headed south. Wind was on the butt so we put the starboard pole out and sailed ◆wing on wing. There was enough wind to have us sailing along at 7 to 8 knots downwind.

Then the quiet and calm of the sea and the enjoyment of sailing took over. The winds were supposed to shift from the northwest to the northeast and drop during the night. We were alone on the sea. We hadn't seen any other boats all day except some shrimp boats earlier. As the sun went down in the west, the full moon rose in the east, giving us a gorgeous but cool evening.

After dinner I crashed aft. Cap woke me up around 11 p.m. to take over for night watch. At 11:30 the wind shifted, then died. Oh, my! I woke Cap up; we rolled up the sails and started the engine. I motored and kept watch until around 4 a.m. We passed a few cruise ships. Cap called them cattle boats. Then I saw a light ahead, a white light, which meant a stern light of a boat. I looked at the radar but didn't see anything. At two miles of separation they finally showed up on the radar. It was another sailboat.

I woke Cap up as the wind started to pick up out of the northeast. We brought in the starboard pole, rolled out the jenny, and started sailing along at 8-plus knots. When I mentioned the other sailboat to Cap, he decided it should be a race. Of course, he and I were the only ones who knew it was a race. He unfurled the mizzen for the extra ½ knot of gain.

I went back to get some sleep. I woke up about sunup and went topside just as we passed the other sailboat about 50 yards away on our starboard side. It was a 46 to 48-foot cutter, a sailboat with two sails in front of the mast.

We had planned to arrive in Fort Pierce about 1:00 p.m., but because of Cap's race with the cutter we arrived at 10:30 a.m. We went into the marina and fueled up. The diesel fuel was expensive. Our 104 gallons cost us $371. We also filled *Lady's* water tanks, since that was free, and it would have cost fuel to run the generator to operate the watermaker.

We considered sailing down to West Palm Beach, another 50 miles, but we would have had to anchor in the dark. Not a good idea, so we found a good spot to anchor just outside Fort Pierce, where Cap cooked our own Thanksgiving dinner.

West Palm Beach

It was at Fort Pierce that I was finally able to stow my gloves, wool socks, and scarves. It was also where I noticed that the toilet seat was no longer cold. Small victories. The temperature was 80 degrees during the day and only fell to 65 degrees at night. I had only been to Florida once before. I was 18 and on my way to visit my parents in Ecuador—they had joined the Peace Corps— and I had a three-hour wait between flights. I thought I would catch a cab and see some Florida sights. When I opened the door to exit the airport, the hot, humid wave of air

that seemed to suck all the air out of my lungs pushed me back inside. I decided to wait inside the air-conditioned terminal for my flight. What a difference 35 years had made to my perspective!

We decided to stay anchored at Fort Pierce until either there was no wind or the wind had stopped blowing from the south-southwest. That wind direction would have had us motoring into the wind. We took the opportunity of a lazy day to clean the boat. Yes, chores again, so not such a lazy day and, well, we didn't clean the entire boat, just the cockpit. It was filthy with dirt and dust from the construction of the marina in Baltimore, so it felt good to get it clean and shiny again.

A beautiful sunrise welcomed us in the morning as we left Fort Pierce on our way to West Palm, where we anchored before dark.

We were up early the next day to make our way to Fort Lauderdale. Seas and winds were calm, so we motored along, with a few squalls blowing through on the way. Cap put sails out during the squalls, which enabled us to motor sail up to 9.5 knots at one time. This was such a contrast to my sailing experience in similar circumstances on the Pacific Coast, when Jack would bring in all the sails during squalls, not put them out.

We entered the channel to Fort Lauderdale in the early afternoon on an incoming tide. A huge container ship was being towed by a tug. At first it was behind us, but then it was going fast enough to pass us. The ship suddenly let go with a deafening blast on the horn that put my heart outside my chest for just a moment as I thought we were doing something wrong. It turned out that it was not blowing the horn at us, but giving a warning blast to some sailboat racers that had come tacking out of the channel.

To my relief, we were still able to make a scheduled bridge opening over the New River.

As Cap motored up the New River to the downtown marina, I got the bumpers and the lines out of what Cap called the trunk and secured them on the starboard side. Cap put the bow thruster down to help us when passing a boat and also when we docked. When we got to the designated piling number provided by the marina management, Cap very slowly maneuvered the *Lady* up to the side. I hopped off with the stern line and secured it to the cleat. Cap then threw me the bow line and I secured it as well. Even with the incoming tide, we made it look fairly easy.

The first thing we did was to drop the main and jenny sail and pack them into sail bags to go to the sailmaker. The sailmaker had not put the ◆telltales on the new main that Cap had just bought, and since we were now close to their location, Cap decided to have them replace the ◆sunbrella on the jenny and do some repairs on it too. They told him that the sail repairs would be completed in three days. Alas! More repair and maintenance expenses for Cap. However, I was very glad that he took such good care of *Lady*.

The marina in the city of Fort Lauderdale was rather unique. In an area with few places to anchor, we were literally downtown, just three blocks from a supermarket and a lot of shops for me to explore. Los Olas Boulevard was just three or four blocks over. Cap told me it was a favorite shopping spot for a lot of the snowbirds from the frozen north.

The marina was basically a channel through the city where boats of all shapes and sizes could be secured to the cement sides of the channel. Small boats, large boats, and big ships motored past us through the channel all day long. The sound of bow thrusters signaled a warning of a big boat making the tight turns on their way to the ocean. The big ships had two tow boats: one in front and one in the back to slow down or stop.

The next morning the sailmaker came and picked up the sails.

Cap hadn't been off the boat in quite a few days, so we decided to walk the half mile to the supermarket. We found a lot of grocery bargains, or what seemed like a lot of bargains, as the bags and our arms were full. By the time we stopped for lunch, Cap's hips and back were really hurting. We got back to the sailboat, where he took his medicine and rested, and I found room to stow all of our purchases.

Being in a marina with unlimited power and water meant it was time for more chores—that is, for me to do some cleaning—especially since we were going to have Cap's friends Phillip and Joanna over for dinner. They were letting us borrow one of their cars for the weekend so we could check additional sales and pick up anything that we may have forgotten.

Just before they arrived, the shore power breaker tripped. Cap had replaced that switch in Baltimore. He went into the engine room and unmounted the switch, letting it hang free. When he did that, everything worked. Since we were expecting company, and Cap was the cook, he left it dangling, so we could enjoy our evening without the noise of the generator. It was a great dinner with a wonderful couple. We made plans to take them on an afternoon sunset sail from Dinner Key in a couple of days.

The next morning, we drove to some marine shops because Cap had decided on a new anchor and was ready to order. He found out that waiting to order until we were in Marathon or Key West was going to work best. We also looked for a replacement switch. We could find nothing that even slightly resembled what we needed.

Returning to the boat, we brought everything aboard. By this time even I was tired from all our running around, so I decided to wait until morning to stow all the dry goods. Since the galley was not in any kind of shape for Cap to cook something, he went into the cockpit with some of his boxed wine and snacks and talked me into joining him to watch the boats go up and down the river. Still not much of a drinker, I had one glass to Cap's three or so, but I did enjoy the boat show.

I got up early to stow away all our purchases and organize the cabinets. When Cap got up, he called the sailmaker. The sails wouldn't be ready for another day and a half, so I decided to clean the decks. Cap went into the engine room to troubleshoot the shore switch. He was able to strip back the insulation on one of the wires to get more of it in the clamp. Once he did that, it started working again. I felt better not seeing the switch hanging free. I was happy that it was now working correctly.

We had made one last trip to get dinghy fuel and visit the supermarket when Phillip came and picked up his car. All we needed were the sails.

On one of my shopping walks, I had found an ice cream place on the other side of the river, so I suggested we take a walk over the bridge. Except for the walk, dishes, and laundry, we had a relaxing day. I did feel a bit odd, even embarrassed, putting the laundry out on the lines in downtown Fort Lauderdale, but it was our only choice for drying clothes.

The sails arrived late in the afternoon. The Jenny had enough of a fix to last another couple of years, and the new main had the telltales. It was too late in the day to put them up, so Cap made gin and tonics, and we again watched the parade of boats going up and down the river. I wasn't a fan of gin, so I always asked that my drink be heavy on the tonic and the key limes, with just a whisper of gin.

In the morning, we put the main sail and the jenny back up where they belonged, took a short walk, then readied the *Lady* for a sail to Miami. Cap started the engine and asked me to cast off the bow line first. We were heading out on a strong outgoing tide. When Cap said he was ready, I cast off the stern line and jumped aboard. I looked behind us to see the huge *Jungle Queen* just rounding the bend. There was no way for Cap to maneuver the sailboat into the middle of the channel in front of the *Jungle Queen*. With a bend in the river just in front of us, the *Jungle Queen* swung its stern toward us as she passed. Cap held the *Lady* up to the wall while in reverse as the current tried to push us down the river. When the *Jungle Queen* engaged her stern thruster, it pushed our stern up against a piling. The outboard engine for the dinghy was on the stern railing that was pushed against the piling. The good news was that it didn't break anything. It did, however, bend the stainless railing, the one I had just polished, and Cap was not happy.

Thankfully, the rest of the motor down the New River was uneventful. As I took the bumpers and lines off the *Lady* and stored them back in the trunk, I took some pictures of the fake snow and Christmas decorations in front of the homes along the way. Once through the drawbridge, we were able to let out some sail and motor sail to get out of the mouth of the river a bit faster.

The sail to Miami was wonderful. We let the sails out and turned off the engine as we turned south. Even in the north current of the ◆Gulf Stream, we were able to sail at 6 to 7 knots. We sailed into the main ship channel of Miami and rolled up the sails when we turned left into Biscayne Bay, which is extremely shallow. We motored along in 8 to 13 feet of water until we found the channel to Dinner Key. The channel was only 8 or 9 feet deep. At times, we had a mere six inches under the keel. Keeping a close eye on the depth gauge as Cap motored was nerve-wracking as he guided the *Lady* through the marina and back out the other side, making a U-turn to get into the anchorage. I was very glad he had done this before. We anchored for the night with only 18 inches under the keel!

Once anchored, we put the dinghy down off the stern deck and into the water. Cap hooked up the outboard, and we lowered it down to the dinghy. He pulled the starter rope. Nothing! I could tell after the first pull that he was in pain. I insisted on pulling the starter rope myself. I pulled and pulled. Nothing! We lifted the outboard back onto the rail and Cap got to work on it. He cleared a clogged fuel line. We lowered the motor back down to the dinghy, and it started on the first pull. We made it into the dinghy dock and walked around to see what was close.

The next day Phillip and Joanna drove down to meet us for a day sail. Cap picked them up at the marina dinghy dock and brought them out to the *Lady*. Phillip had a sailboat, but this was the first time Joanna had ever been sailing. She had sailing jitters and lots of questions. Cap took the dinghy over to a cruiser couple's boat that was anchored next to us. We had asked them to dinghy-sit so we didn't have to lift it aboard or pull it behind us while we were out day-sailing.

As we sailed out of Biscayne channel, we passed by homes on stilts. They were built in Prohibition days as places to drink and gamble. There was no power or water to these homes, but it was obvious that they'd had some updated maintenance. It was real ◆skinny water, as Cap called it, going out through the channel. It was only 8 to 8.5 feet deep, and the *Lady's* keel took 7 feet of that.

Once out of the channel, Cap adjusted our destination for a perfect sail to the wind. What a great sail! Of course, we had to dodge the crazy sport-fishing boats that were flying their kites. They want to head into the wind and don't care who is sailing around them. We had some go right in front of us, expecting us to change our course and miss hitting their kite trailing 75 yards behind them with our mast. Then there were the "go fast" boats zipping around—twenty-eight foot boats with

four 300 horsepower outboards, a total of 1200 horsepower. It seemed a bit much. I was so very glad I was on a sailboat. Joanna and Phillip seemed to be having a wonderful time as well.

We got back to Dinner Key in time for happy hour. Our cruiser neighbors brought our dinghy over and joined us. Cap cooked fajitas, everyone had a few drinks, and we all enjoyed talking about our plans for cruising. Phillip and Joanna stayed late, and we all played Mexican Train dominos, the game that I had only watched when I was on the Pacific Coast. They insisted that I learn to play. It was great fun! I took Joanna and Phillip back to the marina in the dinghy, hoping that I would see them again, perhaps out on the water.

We waited another day for some wind to head down to the Keys. The generator switch, which was also the shore power switch, had failed again when Cap tried to start the generator after our guests left. After breakfast, he got busy trying to figure out what was wrong. He finally decided to wire the generator directly and eliminate the option of having shore power, since we weren't planning on being in a marina until springtime when we got back to Baltimore anyway.

We ran the generator to charge the batteries and got a load of clothes in. Once I had hung the clothes up to dry, we took the dinghy ashore for groceries. When we returned, it was all about getting the sailboat ready for sailing the next day. Cap put the starboard pole up as the wind was forecast to be from behind us. In the meanwhile, I got everything down below secured and ready. The engine was lifted off the dinghy, and the dinghy was lifted up onto the deck. Our normal preparations for a sail were done.

We motored out of the Biscayne Bay channel with the high tide and turned south toward the Keys. We dodged a few more fishing boats flying their kites. Then we let the sails out. It was a great sail until we were slowed down by the edges of the Gulf Stream. We were sailing at 8 to 10 knots when all of a sudden the boat speed read 7.9 knots while the speed over ground was 5.9 knots. That was the effect of the Gulf Stream current.

We stayed outside the reef until we were abreast of Tavernier Key. Cap started the engine and dropped the sails. We motored across the cut in the reef and anchored off the Keys in 8.3 feet of water facing into 20-plus knots of wind. It was a ◆lee shore, so Cap put out extra ◆rode. We were behind the reef so the waves were only 1 to 2 feet. It made for a somewhat bouncy anchorage, but it was okay for sleeping.

Cap woke up in the middle of the night in extreme pain. I heard him in the salon and went in to see what was going on. He told me he was having horrible pain in his lower back, and he knew it was a kidney stone. He'd had this before and knew exactly what the pain felt like. There was nothing I could do, so I went back to sleep. Later he told me he had taken one of his pain pills; he also drank some rum and was was able to go back to sleep. I woke up early, got online, and found a diet for kidney stones. When Cap woke up, he said he'd had success and he felt great.

We would continue our plan to sail south.

We left Tavernier Key a little after 8 a.m. The wind was indeed on the stern, so we put the jenny out on the pole on the starboard side and the main out on the port side. We were once again sailing in skinny water, only 12 to 35 feet deep. We sailed by a green buoy near a sunken boat that had been there long enough to actually be on the charts! We were going 8 to 9 knots, loving this sail, when Cap noticed

another sailboat a couple of miles ahead of us. Of course, it then became a race for him. I watched as Cap let out the mizzen, then adjusted and trimmed the jenny and main sail to get the most speed over ground out of the wind.

By 10:00 a.m. we pulled even with the other boat. We watched him put out his mizzen as we sailed by. When we looked back, the other sailboat had pulled up its main sail. It was a speck in the distance as we turned to anchor behind Boot Key, near Vaca Key and the city of Marathon. The *Lady* was too tall to get under the bridge into the lagoon in Marathon.

Our plan was to be in Marathon for a couple of days visiting friends from the marina in Baltimore. I wanted to go diving. I loved being on the surface of the ocean, but I was ready for the beauty under the surface that I had discovered in Zihuantanejo. And I wanted to take more pictures to share with others, so they, too, could see this truly amazing world. I mentioned to Cap that I had noticed our inflatable dinghy was going flat on one side. It had gotten a leak. On our sail down, Cap had patched it. Once anchored, we found that the patch hadn't fixed the leak, so Cap re-patched it. Now we needed to wait for the epoxy to cure before we could go into town.

I got the laundry and dishes out of the way, then started getting my dive gear accounted for and my camera ready. We left the dinghy at the City Marina dinghy dock to do some shopping. I was stunned that they charged us $10.50 to leave the dinghy at the dock! Cap ordered his new anchor, which we would pick up in Key West. We found a dive shop, but I couldn't get a dive booked during the time that we would be in Marathon. Oh, was I ever disappointed! Oh well, I could still look forward to diving in Key West. By then we had walked over two miles, which had taken us more than four hours. Cap's back and hips were really hurting, so instead of looking for our friends' boat in the marina, we just went back to the *Lady.* Cap had a few stiff drinks to help with his pain and retired early. I stayed up to research diving on Key West.

Expensive dingy dock

The patch seemed to be holding on the dinghy, so we decided to go back into the lagoon and have lunch at the Dockside Restaurant. The winds were strong, 15 to 20 knots, and we were motoring directly into it. The dinghy was flat-bottomed, and even in a moderate chop we would get wet from the spray over the low bow. With the strong winds, we were both getting soaked, but we persevered. Thank heaven the air temperature was in the mid-70s, and we were soon in the lagoon where the waves were less choppy. Once ashore, Cap walked down to our friends' boat, and they decided to join us for lunch. Another couple came down as well, and we had a great time chatting, talking boats, weather, travel plans, and kids.

Key West

Around 8:15 the next morning we hoisted anchor. Well, in truth, Cap pushed the windlass button, and the windlass hoisted the anchor. One boat already had an hour's head start. By the time we had the sails up and were going south, the other boat was 6 or 7 miles ahead. Of course, Cap saw this as another race, an excuse to trim the sails to get the best speed to the wind out of the boat. The other sailboat was a small speck of white on the horizon. The wind in the morning was 15 to 18 knots from the east-northeast, and we were going between 7 and 8 knots. Cap was delighted that the white speck kept getting larger. By noon he was within range, and about 2:00 p.m. we passed him. The wind quit right before we made the turn into Key West. We rolled up the sails and motored into the Key West (KW) anchorage.

The anchorage was quite crowded. Cap had a difficult time placing the anchor. It took three times to get the anchor set to where Cap was happy with the amount of rode and our boat's placement in the anchorage. The weather was forecast to be blowing at 20 to 30 knots, and he wanted to be sure the *Lady* would be safe.

Rain and 35-knot winds from the southwest woke us up early. The wind made for an uneasy anchorage, and we spent the day cleaning the boat from the days at sea.

The next morning, with the hope of more sun, more warmth, and less wind, I did a load of laundry. Then we took the dinghy ashore. This dinghy dock was only $5.50 per day. I still thought that was a lot of money, yet there were an awful lot of dinghys there.

Key West sunset with 'cattle boats' and charters

This being my first time in Key West, Cap felt the need to explain the geography and the culture: Key West was the southernmost city in the continental United States, the people were a bunch of burnt-out hippies from the 60s, and the behavior was a bit risqué. We walked up to Duval Street and window-shopped all of the bars and junk shops. Cap went up to the Garden of Eden bar, a clothing optional place, while I walked farther on to some nicer shops and, of course, to the post office to mail postcards to my mom and my kids. I met up with Cap at one of the waterfront bars for lunch and a few beers for Cap. A local guy was singing. I really liked his singing, but mostly I liked his dog. His dog just lay on the stage, slept, and watched him and the crowd. Yes, I really liked his dog.

The wind was still strong—perhaps up to 25 knots— on our way back to the *Lady,* so the dinghy ride was a soaker. It was fun, but oh so wet, and once wet, I was cold. I was ready to jump in and swim back to the sail-boat, thinking that being in the water I'd be warmer than I was in the dinghy. It was in the mid 70s, but by the time we got back to the *Lady,* I was chilled to the bone. A hot shower later, I found Cap enjoying the evening with a glass of wine in the cockpit.

Key West Christmas

At 2:30 a.m. loud voices woke me up. It was our boat neighbors, Terry and Pam, a very sweet couple from Wisconsin. They were trying to wake us, as the *Lady* and their trawler were side by side, and they were putting bumpers out between our boats. We quickly started the engine and lifted anchor, which was not easy. We thought perhaps the anchor had dragged, but it hadn't. It was just very tough for the windlass to pull it out after being in such high winds for three days. The wind had stopped and the boats had swung differently. We were the last to anchor, so we had to be the ones to move. We re-anchored temporarily farther out, which was no fun in the dark. I was on the bow with a flashlight, illuminating the anchorage so Cap could maneuver through the other boats and find a place to anchor. Once the anchor was back down, even after the adrenaline rush of anchoring in the dark, I went right back to sleep.

Our trawler neighbors

We went into Key West every day. We went to the sunset celebration on Mallory Square just once—been there, done that. I even got Cap to ride a rental bicycle. I thought if he could ride a bike, it might help him get around better with less pain. He had been using my shoulder as a cane, and some days my neck and shoulder really felt it. We rode to the southernmost point of the U.S. just so I could say that I had been there: another "been there, done that." Cap did a pretty good job riding so I bought us both foldable bikes to put on board the *Lady*.

We had Terry and Pam over for a happy hour. Happy hours, I found out, were something that a lot of the cruisers did, and Cap was no exception. Terry told us that they had had the night-time anchor issues three times with three other sailboats in the last three weeks. A sailboat and a trawler swing very differently at anchor, especially with wind and tide changes. I was still embarrassed that it had happened with us though. Cap was always so careful to pick his anchor spot that was respectful of surrounding boats. I was learning so much by watching him.

Key West anchorage at sunset

I was now in the habit of watching all the gauges, and thanks to Cap, I had learned when to turn the generator on to recharge the batteries and when to turn it off. I had recently noticed that the voltage on the batteries was falling lower than usual in the same amount of time, so I asked Cap about it. He checked the water level of the batteries, and they all seemed fine. Another cruiser remarked that he had been putting a quart of water a week in his batteries. Cap had not used a quart of water in the last three months! So, on our next trip into Key West he bought a ◆specific gravity tester (an SGT). The SGT showed that every battery had a dead cell. He ◆equalized the batteries and checked them again. All but one had a weak cell. The batteries were one month over the one-year replacement guarantee, but they did have a three-year prorated warranty. Cap called the vendor to resolve the issue, and we decided that we would go back up to Miami to swap the batteries out with new ones before we headed to the Bahamas and farther south.

In the meantime, Cap had been using my computer to download all sorts of movies and TV shows onto an external memory drive. We were about to leave the U.S. Once we did, we would not be able to get the TV channels. And Cap did enjoy watching his evening TV shows.

After re-anchoring in a different spot for the third time since arriving in Key West, we met Jim and Roberta, cruisers from Wisconsin who had a 45-foot boat named *Chipper*. They came by in their enviable 800-pound, 35 mph dinghy. (The tides and wind had eased us into a little-used channel and the police had come by and asked us to move.) Did I mention that the anchorage was crowded? Someone must have left the anchorage though, because this time Cap found a very nice spot closer to the dinghy dock near our new friends. We met Jim and Roberta that evening for happy hour at The Conch Restaurant and Bar, where I had my *first* "dark and stormy" cocktail. Then I had a second because . . . well, they were two for one. I was over my limit, but we were enjoying the evening. Then we had them over to the *Lady*. It was great fun to chat about travel plans and families. They were eager to hear all about our plans to go down-island to Venezuela. Cap had been to Venezuela before, and he enjoyed filling them in.

The anchor Cap had ordered had been delivered to West Marine. It was a Rocna. After intensive research, he was sure it would be the best anchor for our cruising needs. Luckily, his son had come down for a visit. The timing was perfect; he could carry the anchor from the store to a cab, the cab to the dinghy, and the dinghy to the *Lady*.

I got a spot on a dive boat at last. Although the best time to dive in Florida is in the summer when the clarity of the water is at its best, I just had to go anyway. I wanted to check out Key West under the water. Cap also wanted me to be ready to catch lobsters down island. The more time under the water for me, the better! I was a little disappointed with the first dive. There was not as much living coral as I had expected on what was supposed to be a famous reef. But on the second dive, there was a little more clarity and more life. And oh! The joy of breathing underwater!

A couple from Holland was in my group. I was the only one with a camera, so they took my picture with my own camera, which was nice because I had rarely gotten a picture of myself under the water. I really enjoyed their company. They were respectful of the underwater world, had great buoyancy, didn't touch the coral, and helped me look for interesting things to photograph: fish, coral, and other marvelous surprises. The divemaster had his predetermined route, which was only changed a little by our wanderings. He did stay close to us. The most important thing about the dive was the reminder of how great I felt when I got into the water *and* when I got out of the water! The excitement was so intense for me—the joy, the thrill, and at the same time, the tranquillity.

Key West dive boat

Even though the fish would not stop to have their pictures taken, I was able to bring some pictures up to the surface and onto my computer that reminded me of their world. I certainly needed more practice. I was yearning to plan more dives in Key West.

We enjoyed New Year's Eve in Key West with Jim, Roberta, and a couple who had sailed to Key West from Norway! On New Year's Day, Cap looked at the weather. The forecast was for 30-plus knots of wind the next day. A lot more ditch diggers had come into the anchorage. Cap felt they had anchored too close together. After what had happened to us earlier on in this anchorage, he decided that we would leave and go back up to Marathon. I was disappointed that I would not get any more Key West diving, but I buckled down and readied the boat for travel. We lifted anchor around noon.

Motoring past a shrimp boat

There was little to no wind. We motored all the way up the coast to Marathon. On the way up I changed out the old anchor for the new Rocna anchor. Near Boot Key we dropped the Rocna in nine feet of water. Knowing that high winds were coming, Cap let out an extra 80 feet of chain, and we attached two ◆snubbers: one 20-foot snubber with a backup snubber at around 30 feet. We took the dinghy off the deck, attached the small engine, and secured it with a stainless steel carabiner to the stern of the *Lady*. It would be easier to do it now than in 30-knot winds.

The storm hit about midnight. I had been sleeping great until I felt the boat start to sail back and forth on the anchor and heard the waves slapping onto the hull. That woke Cap up too, and he went topside to check the anchor and snubbers. Using a flashlight, he could see the chain was straight out from the snubbers and the bow of the sailboat. The snubbers and the new anchor seemed to be doing their job of holding us secure.

The wind got up to 41 knots. After Cap came back down below and let me know all was well with the anchor, I fell back into a light sleep in which I felt the movement of the boat and trusted the *Lady* to keep me safe. At first light the wind was still 35 knots. It was sunny and it was cold. We went topside to look around us and found the dinghy missing. The dinghy and engine were nowhere in sight. Our only reliable transportation to shore was gone. Cap called the police. They wanted to meet with us. He then called his insurance company, which asked us to contact the Coast Guard in case it was found. Fortunately, Cap had a spare inflatable dinghy folded up in what he called "the trunk."

We were anchored at the east end of Boot Key about a third of a mile from the entrance to the harbor. It continued to blow 25 knots for the next two days. I cleaned down below and did a load of laundry. Laundry day on a sailboat looks a little different. I have never been one to hang laundry to dry for all to see, even when my kids were young and we were living on a small farm. I can't explain why it bothers me to hang laundry out. In reality, having clean and dry clothes is really nice. And Cap says we do it because *we can*, which is very true. The *Lady* does have a clothes washer. Most all the other cruisers have to go into town and take their laundry to

a laundromat. When I was on Jack's boat, we always had to take laundry into town to wash and dry at a laundromat. So yes, it was convenient having an onboard washer. It just—well, it was still hanging laundry for all to see. I hoped I would get used to it.

When Cap started searching for another ◆RIB (Rigid Inflatable Boat) and engine, I mentioned checking out Craigslist for a used one. I also suggested looking for an electric start engine so he could manage the starting easier than pulling the cord—or having me pull the cord. He found a few engines and dinghys to look at, so he decided to rent a car for a few days.

After two days on the boat, we were all out of fresh vegetables and our garbage was piling up. I wrestled the spare dinghy out from the trunk storage. There was no solid floor, and the inflatable floor was missing. It was in sad shape, but we pumped up the inflatable collars and they held air. When I first stepped into the spare dinghy, my foot sank down into the rubber bottom. I thought I was going to break through to the water underneath, so I quickly sat down on the inflatable collar. The winds had calmed, so we took turns rowing into Marathon. We paid our dinghy dock fee and waited for the rental car to arrive.

Cap had talked to a gentleman in Fort Lauderdale with a 2004 15 hp Yamaha 4-stroke electric start with only three hours on it. It was a 2½ hour drive one way, but we made that our first stop. Cap dickered a bit, and he was able to get it for $1,200—a great deal. Of course, then we had to stop and buy a battery and a battery box for the dinghy.

We got back to Marathon around 10:30 p.m. It was high tide. As it turned out, that was very helpful, because then we only had to get the 120-pound engine down about four feet from street level onto the stern of the dinghy. I slowly walked the engine end over end to the sea wall. Cap made a harness out of a rope for the engine top, tying the other end of the rope to the car, which he had backed a little bit out of the parking spot. I moved the engine over the top of the sea wall while Cap held the rope tight with the car. I then went down into the dinghy, maneuvered it under the hanging engine, and called out to him to drive the car closer, which lowered the engine. I guided it onto the transom and secured it. Then I went back up to the car, retrieved the battery, and carried it down to the dinghy. Cap untied the ropes, locked the car, and came down to the dinghy, where he hooked up the battery and pushed the button. It worked great! The unusual teamwork felt great too.

We motored to the sailboat quietly, compared to our experience with the noisy old two-stroke engine. However, when Cap increased the speed, the dinghy, with no rigid floor, started to fold in the middle. That was not good. We ended up motoring very slowly back to the sailboat.

Cap really wanted either an AB or Caribe brand RIB. He had planned on buying one when we got to Margarita Island, Venezuela. Cap, however, did not like going slow, and with the current combination of engine and dinghy we would have to go slow, so he got back on Craigslist to look again for a dinghy. One had just been advertised in Marathon, and we arranged to look at it the following day.

The rental company picked up the car early the next day, but we had brought our bikes in the dinghy. We rode them the four miles to the dinghy-seller's house. The dinghy was smaller than we were used to. It was only an eight-footer, but it was an RIB, which meant it had a rigid fiberglass floor. It came with an 8 hp Mercury outboard two-stroke for $600, and the seller would deliver it. Cap couldn't resist. The *Lady* now had two motors and two dinghies. As was Cap's tradition, we named the eight-foot RIB "Little Bit" (LB), the electric start engine "Herby," and the smaller two-stroke engine "Stinky." We deflated the spare dinghy and put it back in the trunk storage with Stinky. It is always good to have a spare. Herby could be secured on the back rail and Little Bit secured on the back deck for passages and long sails.

Cap couldn't get marina reservations in Miami. So instead, he made arrangements for us to go back up the New River and into the Fort Lauderdale marina to get the *Lady's* batteries swapped out—all 12 of them. It would be an overnight passage from Marathon. We had a wonderful sail with a 2 to 3 knot assist from the Gulf Stream. We got to the marina at close to 8:00 a.m. Cap unhooked all the batteries by 9:30. Then I lifted them (65 pounds each) out of the battery box and carried them one by one through the boat hallway, up the stairs,

New River, Fort Lauderdale

through the cockpit, over the boat railing, and out onto the dock by 10:00. 12 batteries. Phillip was letting us use his truck again. He arrived around noon. I loaded them into the truck and off to Sam's we went. Cap had called ahead to be sure that the store would have 12 batteries available.

When we got to Sam's, I loaded all the batteries onto a cart, and we trundled over to the tire and battery area. A gentleman came out and tested the batteries with a voltage meter. He pronounced the first three batteries good. Cap told him that the condition of a battery could not be determined by voltage alone and asked if they had a load tester or hydrometer. They did not. We walked over to Walmart, bought a hydrometer for .88 cents, went back to Sam's and showed them how to test the batteries with the hydrometer. I'm not really sure what was being discussed behind the scenes, but the Sam's guy was gone for about 20 minutes. Thankfully, Cap had brought his receipt. When the guy returned, he filled out a form, brought 12 new batteries, took the old ones, and charged Cap $17.00. Wow! I was amazed. I loaded the new batteries into the truck and we went grocery shopping. This would be our last shopping trip in the United States.

Back on the boat, I unloaded the groceries and the 12 batteries out of the back of the truck. One by one, I carried the batteries to the dock, up over the railing of the boat, through the cockpit, down the stairs, through the hallway, and back to the large battery box. Phillip and Joanna came by to pick up their truck, and we took them out to dinner to thank them.

We were up early to ride our bikes to the store for some last-minute provisions. Then we checked out of the marina and moved the boat a short distance to Lake Sylvia, where we anchored. It was time to wait on weather for our passage to the Bahamas. I was so excited. I was planning on diving at least a few times while we were there. We put Little Bit into the water off of the deck, put Herby on, and went to a local restaurant to eat an early dinner. Just as we were getting close to the dinghy dock, I saw a huge speckled black mass in the water. An endangered manatee! Cap slowed the dinghy as it dove under the water and resurfaced with its huge body just below the surface and only its nostrils above the surface. It was an exciting sighting, even though I didn't get a picture.

Getting into and out of Lake Sylvia was tide dependent because the *Lady* needed seven feet or more for her winged keel. We couldn't wait too long as there was a limit on how long a boat could anchor in Lake Sylvia. Cap determined there was a weather window where we could go across the Gulf Stream and get tucked behind a key before any nasty weather coming down from the north arrived. We got the dinghy secured on deck and everything stowed for the passage. Just in time, too, as a local water policeman came by to tell us to leave. Cap informed him we would be leaving with the high tide at 10:00 a.m.

0   100   200 miles

Fort Lauderdale

Berry Islands

The
Bahamas

Virgin
Islands

Guadalupe

Margarita
Venezuela

200   300 miles

Chapter 5

Sailing to Bahamas and Saint Thomas, United States Virgin Islands

In the beginning, the wind was perfect for a fast sail across the Gulf Stream toward the Bahamas. At first, the sailboat's movement felt like riding a gentle, loping horse. As we got farther away from the U.S. and into the Gulf Stream, the gentle lope became a consistent bow dive into the waves, with a few twists now and again. The seas became even more confused as the winds shifted. Just before dark, I started hearing a scraping noise every time the bow got buried forward into the water. We checked out the anchors. With the extreme motion of the passage, the spare anchor had shifted.

At first, Cap was insistent that he go forward to tie the anchor down. I had to raise my voice a little before he finally conceded. I had good reasons for thinking I was best for the job at hand. My balance and agility were far better than his, and the likelihood of success with no negative results was higher. If I fell over-board, I could swim longer than he could, and he would be the best to maneuver the boat to get me. Most important, I was saving myself the stress of watching him up on the bow with the waves hitting him. There was no question in my mind that I could have maneuvered the

boat to get him if he were to fall overboard, but he probably could not stay afloat long enough even with a life ring. So, just for a moment, I got to feel like I was out at sea catching Alaska crab like the guys on the reality show *Deadliest Catch*, albeit on a much, much, smaller scale.

Cap started the knot he wanted me to use and I slowly, keeping very low to the deck, made my way up the port side of the boat. It took me a little longer than I expected, and I did lose my favorite hat in the process, but I secured the anchor so it no longer scraped when the bow was buried in the ocean waves. I can't say it was fun—I got soaked—but it was exhilarating. I came back to the cockpit feeling very accomplished and then went down below for a hot shower and some dry clothes. How about that! In the middle of a passage, a hot shower! The continuous shifting movements of the sailboat while I was in the shower did make standing a bit difficult, but still, I felt so very lucky.

I have mentioned that Cap likes to go fast. Fast is a relative term when it comes to small sailboats. Most of my sailing in Jack's boat had been between 3 to 5 knots (3.45 miles per hour to 5.75 miles per hour). Much of our sailing on Cap's boat had been between 6 and 9 knots: 6.90 mph to 10.36 mph. Cap preferred 9 knots, but that speed was always dependent on wind, wind direction, and seas.

Cap planned on a conservative 6 knots for our 20-hour passage to the Bahamas. That would give us enough time to cross the Gulf Stream before the big cold front from the north blew through with expected winds of 35 knots. Plus, we would be able to make the turn south along the Bahamas Bank during daylight hours. The Bahamas Bank is an extremely shallow area between the islands where the water depth averages only 8 to 9 feet. With the *Lady's* keel at 7', Cap did not want to cross the area at night or in 35 knot winds. Our current speed during the daylight hours, even with rough seas, was 8 to 9 knots. If we kept up that speed, we would arrive way too early to the Bahamas Bank.

Cap reduced sail, but even with that attempt to delay us, it seemed best that we change course and take a longer route, the course that the cruise ships take. Once it got dark, the skies and seas were lit up with a parade of cruise ships passing us on their way to the Bahamas and Saint Thomas or returning to Fort Lauderdale. Cap was not feeling well again—another kidney stone—so I tried to let him sleep by taking more of the night shift. When the boat was in bumpy and confused seas, the motion in the fore and aft cabin was a lot more vigorous than in the center of the boat. He could not sleep, so we took turns at the wheel watching the "cattle boat" parade.

Cap took the helm about 4:30 a.m. just as the last cruise ship passed. Lightning in the clouds north of us confirmed that the front was approaching. I went down below and got a little sleep while Cap reefed all the sails down for the forecasted blow. He made the turn south about 5:00 a.m. After the turn, the seas were calm with 15 knots of wind. I woke up and took over what turned out to be a wonderful sail while Cap finally got some sleep. When he got up, the front had arrived. All we could see behind us was the black wall of clouds. In just minutes, the wall of weather caught up and enveloped us. The wind shifted 120 degrees and the temperature

dropped 20 degrees. Wind speed picked up to 25 knots, and it started raining hard. We were cruising south along the Berry Islands. Cap checked his maps and found a small inlet where we could duck in behind Frozen Cay. We motored through the inlet, anchored in 12 feet of water and prepared the topside for a blow by putting anything that could be blown away into storage. After securing everything, we took a few minutes to look around. We were in a cluster of very small islands that looked to be completely uninhabited.

I didn't sleep well behind the reef. The wind was 25 knots all night, and it rained and rained. When the tide was running out of the small bay, there was a current of at least a knot or two that had the sailboat sideways to the inlet. In addition to the current, the waves were coming in around the reef and rolling the boat from side to side. In the morning Cap went topside to check the new Rocna anchor and the snubbers. The primary snubber was stretching like a rubber band in the wind, but the anchor was holding well.

The wind increased to 30 knots, and there was more rain. We waited. We watched some of the movies and TV programs that Cap had downloaded. I went topside every once in a while to watch the rain and the wind. When the rain stopped briefly, I took a picture or two of the waves hitting the outside reef.

I wasn't sure what was giving me an uneasy feeling about waiting out this storm where we were. Perhaps I was worried about getting out of the narrow inlet where we had taken refuge from the storm. And indeed, motoring out of the inlet did have its scary moments. The seas just outside the small bay were still choppy, high, and confused from the previous strong winds. Cap checked the weather. The rain was over, and we would have good winds to sail down to Chub Cay, so we lifted anchor and began motoring out of the inlet at almost 6 knots. As we were motoring out of the inlet, the bow of the *Lady* was buried in a huge breaker that stopped her in her tracks,—zero speed over ground—and then quickly turned her sideways at the mercy of the oncoming waves for what seemed like an eternity. Cap increased engine speed and turned her sharply to get the bow pointed back out to the open sea. It was certainly a scary episode in that uninhabited area, a vivid reminder that we were truly on our own out there.

We had a wonderful, albeit bumpy, sail down to Chub Cay, Bahamas. Cap was planning on

Chub Cay, Bahamas

checking into the Bahamas in the morning. I was excited, as I was ready for more diving. After a quiet and peaceful sleep, we took Little Bit and Herby off the deck and into the water. I stayed on the *Lady* while Cap took Little Bit into town with all our papers. An hour later, Cap came back. To check in, we would have to go into the marina dock for 20 minutes, which would cost an extra $100.00 in addition to the $300.00 check in. "No way!" said Cap. We decided to wait a day, then sail over to Nassau to check in. It would still cost $300, but not the additional $100 to tie up to the dock for a mere 20 minutes.

We started working on chores. The front head had not been working for a couple of days, so Cap decided that would be his chore for the day. He tried using a plunger to no avail, so he started taking the thing apart. The 1½ inch diameter five-foot hose had completely closed up with what looked like concrete. Of course, there was no Home Depot around to buy a pipe snake or even another piece of hose, so Cap found a piece of old ◆lifeline—he had put one new lifeline up during the summer and had kept some of the old—and used it as a pipe snake while flushing it with water. After three and a half hours of painstaking snaking with a lifeline (mostly by Cap, I admit), all of the concrete inside the pipe had been broken out. Cap put it all back together and it worked. I cleaned and disinfected the front head, we both took showers, and we relaxed with a well-deserved happy hour drink.

We woke up to a completely calm morning. There was a full moon still in the sky, and the water was as clear as crystal. Cap checked the short-term weather forecast. If we waited one day, we would be able to sail, not motor, over to Nassau. He then decided to send off for a longer-term weather file. He saw a three or four day weather window with the wind from the north. That was unusual. He downloaded a few more weather files and made a decision: in the morning we would make the run, sailing east as far as we could with the north winds, then turning south to sail with the forecast east winds. From Chub Cay, Bahamas, Saint

Thomas and the rest of the Virgin Islands were approximately 400 miles east and then then approximately 400 miles south. The winds this time of year were also mostly from the east, so it just made sense. We were in a sailboat, and it was possible that we could sail to our next destination, Saint Thomas. Now I'm not going to lie; I was also very disappointed. I had so wanted to go diving in the Bahamas, but sailing out on the ocean was superior to motoring. The passage of around 835 nautical miles would take us about 6 days.

We stowed everything we could and readied for the passage the evening before. We were up early, raised the anchor, and got out of Chub Bay with good winds. Thus began our long passage. The first few days were uneventful, with great sailing, but absolutely miserable. Cap forgot to look at sea height in the forecast, and we were getting tipped constantly from the up to 12-foot waves, which at short intervals were also slapping the side of the boat. I took my watch from 9:00 p.m. to 1:00 a.m., but there was no sleeping, even though we both tried.

A flying fish landed on our deck. I spotted it too late to save it. We saw hundreds of them during the day, skipping and gliding through the air from the top of one wave to another. We both were so tired that in the afternoons, we spent time watching the radar, Cap's TV programs on my computer, and trying to take turns napping on the settee.

The third day out we decided to try our luck at catching a fish. We put one of the lures that I had bought at the Annapolis Boat Show on the fishing pole, but all we caught was sargasso seaweed. The next day we were down below on the settee, half watching the radar, half watching a movie, and sailing along at 9 knots with the waves knocking us from side to side, when all of a sudden we heard a loud *zinggg*! What was *that*? Up to the cockpit we hustled. I started rolling up the sails, but the boat was still going forward. When Cap got to the pole, there was only 100 feet of line left on the reel. "Start the engine! Put it in reverse!" Cap hollered. Our forward motion was stopped, but that started an even more horrendous roll of the boat from side to side. I was worried. We must have hooked a monster. What in the underwater world were we pulling up to the boat? Cap would pull in 100 feet of line, and then the fish would take 100 feet out. For over an hour we were at the mercy of the waves that rocked the boat while we tried to bring this unknown fish to the surface. It went around the back of the boat and up the other side. We scrambled around, passing the fishing pole

around the stays. Then we saw it! An incredible fish—vibrant yellow, green, blue and gold! I yearned to jump in and get underwater photos. It was a mahi-mahi.

Cap got the 120-pound test line close enough for me to grab. Cap gaffed the fish but couldn't lift him into the cockpit. I took the gaff handle and got him aboard. I'm not sure how I did it, but there he was! Aboard and in the cockpit. He was a giant. So beautiful! He thrashed and splattered blood all over the cockpit and us. Cap used a squirt bottle with alcohol to spray his gills and put him out. We rested a few minutes before Cap went below to sharpen the fillet knife. He also brought up a tape measure. The fish was 60 inches to the tip of his tail. We guessed his weight to be 35 to 40 pounds.

Cap got us sailing back on our course line to Saint Thomas while I put the cockpit table up and lifted the mahi mahi onto it. Having the sails up helped mitigate the tossing from side to side that we had put up with for the last hour and a half. I watched as Cap began to fillet our catch. I asked if I could help, then took over the job of filleting. We had a great dinner that night, as well as a lot of fillets in the freezer.

I lost track of the the day, the date, even what time it was. Except for the fact that both of us were very tired because of the inability to sleep, the sailing was terrific. We had minimal engine time and up to 11 knots boat speed, although the waves made the passage pretty rocky. I did believe that when we got to land again, I would walk funny and have the land sickness I had after my months on Jack's sailboat.

I asked Cap the next morning if we were going to be able to fish more as we got farther down the islands. He said we would, but that mahi-mahi fishing was best out in the Atlantic. Nevertheless, I let the lure out, thinking that fresh mahi-mahi again or tuna for dinner, plus a little more in the freezer wouldn't hurt. But I thought we might not catch anything at all. I went back down below. We were sailing along between 7 to 9 knots, depending on gusts, and we were just about ready to watch another TV episode, when *zinggg*! We were quicker this time at recognizing the sound and getting up to the cockpit. Cap went to the pole as I brought sails in, started the engine, turned auto pilot off…into reverse…turning left…forward….no, the other left (oops)…anyway, starboard. Then Cap gave me the pole.

This fish, too, did not want to come aboard. It put up a valiant effort, a few ups and a few runs, but it was not nearly as difficult as the monster from yesterday. It was half an hour before I had her to the side of the boat so Cap could gaff her. We got her into the cockpit. It was a female mahi-mahi about 47 inches long, another beautiful fish. Cap got the sailboat back on course again, sailing along at 8.5 knots in 20-plus knots of wind, as I proceeded to clean and fillet the fish in the bouncing cockpit. I was getting better at filleting with sharp knives, even with the boat going 8 knots and waves tipping us to the side. If I stop to think about it, perhaps it was because I didn't want to waste any of the precious meat that we took from these beautiful fish, and while it may sound corny to some, I lifted up a prayer when I threw the skeletal remains back into the water, giving thanks to the ocean for sharing with us. We cleaned the fish towel by dragging it behind the boat. Our freezers were now full. I did have to take some of Cap's happy hour ice out of the freezer to fit all the fillets in, but he was not too concerned, since on passages he would not drink anyway. We were done fishing for a while.

We had been at sea for five days, now going on six. About 24 hours out of Saint Thomas we truly had some of the best sailing. We had put the starboard pole up because the winds were from the north, northwest. For seven hours we were sailing fast enough for Cap to think he might get a magic 200-mile sailing day. The *Lady* hit 11.1 knots surfing down the waves. By afternoon, the winds had decreased and we were sailing between 7 and 8 knots. So much for the 200-mile day. But I did get a better feel for why Cap always wanted to go fast: that speed over the water in a sailboat was exhilarating.

Early the next morning we could make out the island of Saint Thomas through the early morning squall. By noon, we had rolled up the sails and were motoring into the Charlotte Amalie harbor. We tried catching up on our lost sleep that first day, but the list of things to do kept getting longer, so we gave up and went into town.

One of the first things on the to-do list was to buy a replacement wi-fi antenna so we could get the Internet on the sailboat. Cap had an older one that wasn't working well. The local Internet shop sold Internet time by the number of hours or days. If we had a wi-fi antenna, we would be able to get Internet on the boat and not have to go into town to the Internet cafe. We also needed to find a replacement hose for the watermaker before we could make enough water to do our loads of laundry.

We took Little Bit (LB) off the deck, got the smaller engine (Stinky) out of the trunk and onto the LB transom, and motored in to the dinghy dock. The dinghy dock here was also where some of the smaller foot ferries docked, so we had to be careful where we tied up. We then took what Cap called the dollar safari bus up to the TuTu Park Mall. Cap called it the dollar safari bus because it was for the locals. Last year the trip had only cost him $1.00 each way. We went to pay the driver $2.00 for both of us and found that they had raised their prices since Cap was here last year. It was now $2.00 each. The same type of trucks with covered seats in the back also worked as the cruise ship transports for $5.00 each from the cruise ship dock to downtown and then $5.00 again for the return trip. There was no signage to be able to tell the difference between the safari and cruise ship buses. We just had to look to see if there were locals or what looked like cruise ship people on board before we hopped on! I also noted that the cars and buses drove on the wrong side of the road. Of course, the wrong side was relative to where I came from: the United States, where we drive on the right side of the road. In Saint Thomas cars and buses drive on the left side.

Saint Thomas

We bought some bread and a new wi-fi antenna from a chain store and caught the bus back to the dinghy dock area. The view from the top of the hill was beautiful. I spent some time walking around in the alley shops frequented by the cruise ship people, while Cap walked to one of the Internet shops. It seems he had picked up a virus on his computer and wanted some help

Hassel Island Bay

getting rid of it. Back at the *Lady*, Cap gave his new antenna a try. It didn't work like he wanted. I packaged it back up so we could return it. Saint Thomas was still in the United States, and it had Office Max, Home Depot, K-Mart, Radio Shack, Wendy's, and McDonald's. It seemed odd after all those miles of sailing to get away from "civilization." Every night, the usual sound of waves gently lapping the sides of the boat was disrupted three or four times by the wail of sirens from the island. I have no idea if they were police or fire sirens, but I found it unsettling that it happened so often—and every night! I was very glad to be on a sailboat in the middle of the harbor and not on shore.

I was learning that even what we thought would be the simplest of chores could take all day or more here in the islands. A stop at a dive shop was high on my priority list, and I got signed up for a two-tank dive in a couple of days. I was very excited. We had taken in the water-maker hose that needed replacing and asked them if they knew where we might get a new hose made. They suggested a guy across the harbor, so we got in LB and motored over to the shop. A gentleman who was there said he couldn't help, but there was a watermaker guy upstairs. We thought we had gotten lucky. Up the stairs we went. The door was locked. It was afternoon by this time, so we thought we would come over early the next day. To make a much longer story short: we checked for two days, and no one ever showed up upstairs in the building with the locked door. We asked around again, and this time the people we asked sent us back to the *other* side of the harbor and up a rickety dock to a rigging shop. The gentleman there said they could do it, but only at their other shop. He gave directions. After 30 minutes of walking and not finding it, we started to double back. Cap's legs were just about to give out when a guy stuck his head out of a door and asked if we were looking for a hose. The hose itself only took a half hour for them to duplicate and cost $63.00. I convinced Cap to have the old hose fitted with another part so we would have an emergency spare. Back at the sailboat, Cap put the new hose on, and we motored over to a bay off Hassel Island and anchored. The water was cleaner in Hassel Island Bay and we were getting low on water.

Saint Thomas marina anchorage from Hassel Island Bay

We made some water, and the next morning we did two loads of laundry. From Hassel Bay we took LB over to the chain store on the far side of Charlotte Amalie, and Cap returned the wi-fi antenna he'd bought and got a different one that he thought might be better. When we got back to the *Lady*, we did a third load of laundry. In the afternoon, after all but one load of laundry was dried, we motored back to the main Charlotte Amalie anchorage. Cap motored around the anchorage while I hooked up the new antenna, trying to find the best signal. We still could not get the wi-fi to work properly, so we anchored the *Lady* and took LB into town. Cap went to the Internet shop, and I did a little more downtown alley shopping. Back at the boat, Cap made happy hour drinks, followed by a wonderful lamb dinner with salad. Having an onboard gourmet chef was a definite plus.

I explored the Saturday market, where I bought some postcards and towels for my mom and my kids. My computer keyboard had finally decided it had had enough. I kept telling Cap that he had to type more gently when he used it, but to no avail. We went into the Internet shop, and I ordered a new one online. We could use the shop as a delivery address, which was awesome. Cap also took back all the antennas he'd bought on the island and ordered a super powerful one online. Now we just had to wait for these two things to arrive.

After all our days of walking, Cap's knee decided to buckle on our way back to the dinghy dock, and he fell onto the side of the road, where he almost rolled out into the street. We had had enough for another day.

I wanted to try to get Cap's knee stronger, so I suggested we take the bikes into town. The next day we rode along the waterfront from the cruise ship dock at one end of the bay, almost to the cruise ship dock at the other end of the bay and back. While it felt great to be back on the bikes, we found that Saint Thomas was really not the best place to ride bikes. It was a far cry from Key West, which is super bike friendly. Although we hadn't ridden in two weeks, we were both able to jump on and enjoy the exercise.

Cap took me to the dive shop early the next morning for my two-tank dive. I had gathered all my gear together the night before so I would be ready. I had bought a neoprene-skin dive hood to help me stay warm and even a new mask with prescription lenses. I was so very excited. While everyone else was in shorties, I had my 3-mil full wetsuit on. Oh well. At least I knew I would be warm on my second dive.

It felt so great to be under the water, even if there were only little fish and eels to be seen. What an incredibly beautiful world the fish have, and how wonderful I felt when I was in their world. On every dive I tried to get pictures that captured the beauty and awe that I felt, so I could share my joy with my children and others. I just needed to keep diving.

The next day we went shopping again for some last-minute food provisions and additional alcohol of the happy hour variety. On our way back we got caught in a powerful tropical downpour. Over an inch of water was running down the roads, which could not drain fast enough to prevent lakes from developing in the streets. Thankfully, we had brought our large waterproof backpacks, which we almost always had with us. We ducked into the Internet cafe to finalize my new computer order and to get out of the rain for a minute.

We were up early planning to sail to Saint John for a couple of days when we heard a knock on the hull. One of the other cruisers had stopped to tell us our dinghy (LB) was upside down. We had been securing it to the side of the *Lady* instead of bringing it on deck every night. We rushed out and hauled LB up onto the stern. I pumped up the portside tube, which had completely deflated. We took Stinky off the transom of LB and secured it to the rail.

Cap knew what to do. Apparently this was not the first time he had an outboard take a bath in salt water. He removed the plugs, flushed them with fresh water, sprayed them with WD-40, then replaced them. After ten or so pulls, Stinky started. Little Bit was holding air, so we put it back in the water and put Stinky back onto the transom. Stinky was running smoothly. Our neighbors came by to tell us they had seen that one side of our dinghy had deflated, and then they had seen some larger boat waves flip it over. We had had two life jackets in LB, and Cap's flip-flops were inside when it flipped. They had floated off when the dinghy flipped. We spent the rest of the morning motoring LB around, searching the area. We recovered one sandal and one life jacket. After all the excitement, we decided to wait until the next day to sail or motor over to Saint John. And we decided to sail around to some of the other British and U.S. Virgin Islands, since we had ten days before my computer and Cap's antenna would be delivered to Saint Thomas.

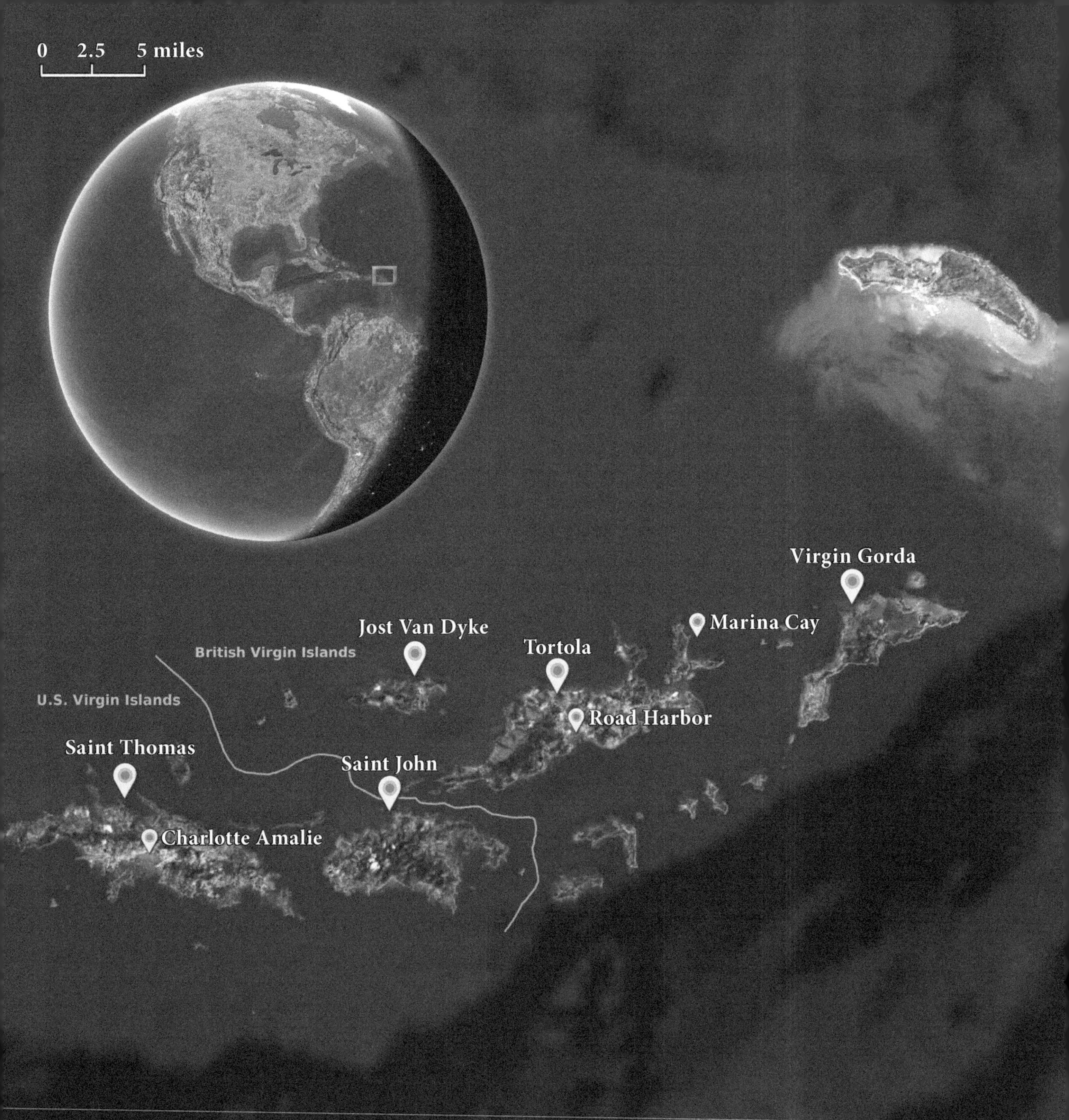

0   2.5   5 miles

Virgin Gorda

Marina Cay

Jost Van Dyke

British Virgin Islands

Tortola

U.S. Virgin Islands

Road Harbor

Saint Thomas

Saint John

Charlotte Amalie

Chapter 6
British Virgin Islands

We started out around 7:30 in the morning for Saint John, but as we got closer, Cap saw that with the wind strength and direction, we could sail quite comfortably to Jost Van Dyke and check in to the British Virgin Islands (the BVI's) there—another change of plans because we were on a sailboat.

We had a great sail, albeit short. We were anchored at Great Harbour, Jost Van Dyke and checked into the BVI's before noon. We did have a bit of a hassle with my 20-gauge shotgun. Of course we declared it, but the customs agent was not sure what to do. At first, he wanted us to surrender it until we left. No problem. Then he stated he would just seal the gun case. Then he called the local police. Then he asked us to bring the shotgun to his office. We went back to the boat and got the gun and the case.

The policeman arrived. He said we had to give him the gun until we left. "No problem," we repeated. The policeman called the home office on Tortola. They decided that we just had to secure the gun. He asked if we had a safe. Cap said we did. They told us to make sure the gun was secure and safe. We brought it back to the boat with a customs seal. Cap did not tell them that the safe was only 24 by 24 inches, far too small for the shotgun. Hey! They didn't ask!

The beach at Jost Van Dyke

Cap had a thick book filled with flags he had purchased many years prior. It listed all the different national flags. After I retrieved the BVI flag, and raised it in the spreader, we went back ashore and took a walk along the road, asking about diving for lobster. We found out that we'd need to get a permit from the fisheries department in Road Harbour on the island of Tortola. Our next stop was the famous Foxy's bar, where we decided that we would spend some of our happy hour time in the evening. As we walked back to the dinghy dock on the beach, I kept hearing screaming noises coming from behind the buildings. A lot of screaming. My eyes searched the hillsides. Sure enough, noisy white goats and their kids covered the hills.

We went back to the sailboat. Cap had been telling me about the charter boats in the BVI's. He was convinced that the charter companies would rent a boat to just about anyone, whether or not they had the skills to anchor properly. Cap called it "afternoon entertainment." But really,

he just wanted to be sure we stayed aboard the *Lady* until any charters had anchored, so he would feel comfortable going to Foxy's for the evening. He had a lot of money invested in his boat, and he did not like to have the charter boats anchor near the *Lady*. Having been in this anchorage before, Cap knew the holding was not the best. Plus, in some areas, it was very deep. Because we had gotten to the anchorage early, he found a great spot in about 15 feet of water with a small cluster of cruisers around us, anchored with proper spacing.

Around 3:30 in the afternoon, I was down below writing on my computer, and Cap was in the cockpit starting his happy hour a bit early, when he called out for me to come topside; the show had begun. For the next two hours, we watched 10 to 12 charter boats attempt to anchor, some of them seven times or more. Sometimes they even dropped their anchor on

top of the next boat's anchor. I thought Cap had been exaggerating, but this was amazing and for me, a bit stressful to watch. On Jack's boat on the Pacific Coast and now on Cap's boat, I always watched carefully how and why they chose their anchor spots. I was no expert, but even with my limited experience, I could tell these people were making a mess of anchoring. Several charters tried, but none were able to break into our anchorage field of cruisers.

When it got dark, and we were fairly sure no other charters would be scurrying into the anchorage, we went ashore to Foxy's. Going ashore for happy hour felt like going out for a fancy dinner, so I dressed in what I felt was appropriate. Remember, I was not a big drinker. Cap had been encouraging me to have drinks during happy hours on the boat, but I didn't always put alcohol in my drinks. So at Foxy's, since I had never had one, I had a "painkiller." Cap reveled in the fact that I had not only one, but two! Then some cruiser bought me a "Friggin in the Riggin." I had had enough. We had not had dinner, so we decided to go back to the boat. We got to the dinghy dock, and Cap fell into the water trying to crawl into the dinghy. The crawling into the dinghy was always the way he got into the dinghy from a dinghy dock, so that was nothing new, but falling into the water was. Luckily the water was not too deep. He could stand up and roll over the inflatable tubes into the dinghy. It was not pretty, but he got it done. By then, I was not feeling well at all. When we got back to the *Lady*, I took a hot shower and went to sleep.

The next morning, I felt much better. We started talking about our evening. I told Cap I was very happy that I had been able to keep my shawl on at all times. So far, I had won that battle: I had not started wearing real cruiser coats like windbreakers when we went ashore for a fancy time. I said I was very happy that I had not fed the fish (thrown-up). And, I added wryly, I was very happy that I hadn't gone for a swim. As I was laughing at his evening "swim" that had left him standing in water at the dinghy dock, Cap pointed out that I had pulled on the dinghy line while he was holding onto the dock. I didn't remember doing that at all. That, he said, was what made him lose his balance, as he repeated three times, "I'm going in…I'm going in…I'm going in," and then once ,"I'm in." To his credit, he didn't get mad at me or tell me it was my fault until morning. To my credit, I did not start laughing about his slow-motion roll until morning when I knew he was just fine, and I was feeling better.

I told myself that I needed to be on guard now. I had always had fun testing my balancing skills, walking along the inflatables while getting in and out of the dinghy. Cap had said many, many times that it was only a matter of time before I went for a swim. Perhaps now, it would be sooner rather than later. Anyway, we had corned beef and hash for breakfast. There was a lot of leftover corned beef that was supposed to have been our dinner the previous night.

After breakfast, we lifted anchor and motored over to Little Harbour on Jost Van Dyke. Since there were only light winds, we put the towing harness on Little Bit rather than lifting it on deck for the short trip. We anchored among the moorings—$25.00 for those who did not know how to anchor—and took Little Bit into Sydney's Peace and Love Bar and Restaurant to look around. We chatted with an island lady who welcomed us and asked if she could help us. There was a small shopping area, so I went over to look around while Cap took advantage of the self-service bar. He had already had two rum punches by the time I returned from shopping. We looked at the menu and decided to have dinner ashore at Sydney's later.

View from Little Harbor

Peace and Love Bar, Little Harbor

We went back to the boat as some charter boats (both monohull and catamarans) were coming in to secure a mooring for the night. We started the generator, did two loads of laundry, and made some water. The new batteries seemed to be doing well so far. I was topside relaxing after hanging the laundry when a catamaran came in and tried to pick up a mooring. I called to Cap to come and watch the entertainment. He grabbed a beer and came up just as a 48-foot cat attempted to grab the mooring. Five or six people were up on the bow. Cap called this "grabbing a mooring by committee." The captain of the cat was trying to have them grab the mooring while he was motoring downwind. They were going way too fast, and the bow committee missed snagging the mooring. They spun around and tried again with the wind at their beam. Missed again. They left the harbour. A smaller catamaran came in and began trying to get a different mooring. After a few misses, they finally motored into the wind slowly enough for the woman on the bow to grab it. I was getting a kick

Lady

Charter boat grabbing a mooring

out of watching them, but I was mostly learning by observation what *not* to do. We went into the restaurant after the evening entertainment was over. I had a large lobster, and Cap had the pig roast. It was so nice to eat out and not have to clean up the galley after Cap cooked. And there were no dishes to wash.

We left Little Harbour in the late morning after a leisurely tea with a cinnamon streusel muffin made from my newest favorite muffin mix, which I'd found at the store in Saint Thomas. We were sailing for the back side of Peter Island. We tried to plan our destination so we could sail with the winds rather than motoring. Even though we tacked a few times, we couldn't make it to Peter Island and headed to Road Harbour instead to anchor for the night.

There was really no place to anchor at Road Harbour, where we saw hundreds of cats waiting in the marina to be chartered! Hundreds! Wow, just wow. We then sailed through some rain squalls over to Norman Island, where we anchored in Money Bay. Cap did a few boat chores, and I did some writing. The anchorage was very deep with beautiful water. A deep anchorage usually meant that there would be only cruisers around and no charter boats. Cap wanted to snorkel in The Indians, an uninhabited island chain, rather than in Money Bay, so we left early while having tea and left-over streusel muffins in the cockpit.

Motoring out of Little Harbour towing Little Bit

Road Harbour charter catamarans

Cap did not like mooring balls, as he felt he could not trust the maintenance and therefore the holding integrity of the mooring, but there was no anchoring at The Indians. Picking up a mooring ball was the only way we would be able to snorkel around the area. We were pretty lucky: just as we arrived, a cat left. Cap had remembered lots of mooring balls here, yet now there were only three.

Sailing thee British Virgin Islands

So, to whom do we give the credit for getting the mooring ball? Both of us. It was a team effort. I'd had a little experience on Jack's boat, but I was more than a little nervous. The neighboring boat was keeping a watchful eye, and I didn't want us to look like the rookies we had been laughing at the previous nights. I got it on the second try! Cap was maneuvering so very slowly right toward it, that it really would have been difficult for me to miss. So I think what I'm saying is that just about anyone can grab a mooring ball (even me) when the boat is in the right place at the right time and going very, very slowly. We went down below, finished our tea, dug out our masks, snorkels, and fins, and over the side we went into the warm water.

The Indians

Snorkeling was never really something I enjoyed, even as a kid. And now, I would really rather be diving. But I was in the water, it was warm, and it was beautiful. There was little to no current and no wave action. The water was 40 to 50 feet deep, yet we could somewhat see the bottom. The yellow-tailed snappers were almost too friendly. I wondered if people fed them. I hoped not. We finished our snorkel/swim, and in typical Cap fashion he had us check the bottom of the boat to see if it was in need of a scraping. It was in really good condition with only a few barnacles on the propeller.

The Indians

We showered, and by the time we left The Indians, there were four or five boats circling, waiting for one of the mooring balls. We had a great sail, tacking up the Sir Francis Drake Channel to Marina Cay. Cap had been telling me of a famous dive site in the BVI's: the wreck of the Royal Mail Ship (RMS) Rhone. Once we anchored in Marina Cay, we were able to get online using Cap's old antenna, and I found a dive boat out of Virgin Gorda Sound for a two-tank dive on the Rhone. Was I ever so excited at the opportunity! We planned to head to Virgin Gorda Sound the next day so I could meet them for the dive early on Wednesday. I hopped over the side and snorkeled around a bit as Cap had requested a picture of his anchor in the sand.

Between three and four in the afternoon, the charter boats started racing into the small Marina Cay anchorage to pick up a mooring ball. Once the mooring balls were all picked up, there were still charters trying to anchor. A catamaran was anchoring by committee between two mono-hulls. Monohulls swing differently than cata-marans in the wind. When they couldn't seem to find a good spot, they just anchored anyway and put out all their bumpers along both sides. After they had put the bumpers out, they all piled into their dinghy and motored up to the dinghy dock to go to the bar, a seemingly reck-less behavior that I could not understand. This kind of behavior seemed to centered on sailing around, finding the bars, and drinking on each island.

Marina Cay anchorage from the bar

The Rocna anchor, Marina Cay

Anchoring by committee

Putting bumpers out

We watched as a different catamaran tried to drop anchor in 35 feet of water. After three to four tries, a captain on another boat from the same charter company took a dinghy over to help them. (The smarter of the charter boat crowd hire a captain for the duration of their charter.) Another monohull made four tries before hooking something at the rear of the mooring field. Then a charter monohull came motoring very fast, too fast, through the anchorage, trying to find a spot to anchor since all the moorings were taken. He ended up running the sailboat aground. He backed off at full speed and almost backed into the reef behind him. He raced through the anchorage one more time and then decided to motor off to a different anchorage. By 5:30 p.m. the anchorage had quieted, and we breathed a sigh of relief. This was a very different atmosphere, such a very different way of life, from what I had experienced in my travels on the Pacific Coast with Jack.

When Cap was sure that all of the entertainment was over, we got into Little Bit and went ashore to Pussers restaurant and bar. There was live music, the music was loud, it was crowded, and drinks were flowing. Cap was having a great time. We got back to the dinghy dock to find that a young woman had fallen into the water; I wasn't sure if she had fallen off the dinghy or off the dock. She was lucky, too, that the water was only waist high. Both she and her husband were smiling

After the charter crowd left around ten the next morning, we moved the *Lady* closer to the island for Internet access. The forecasted wind was supposed to be high—25-plus knots from the east. We would have had to motor into six to ten-foot seas to get to Virgin Gorda, so we decided to stay in Marina Cay on Tortola and get some chores done. The dive boat would not be going out in these winds anyway. We took garbage ashore (It cost $2 a bag.), and I bought some more postcards. We saw a squall coming and rushed back to the boat in time to close the hatches. The weather was warm, and keeping the hatches open as much as possible helped it stay cooler down below. About that time six to eight catamarans and a few monohulls came into the anchorage. There were only a few mooring balls left, which meant by that by four o'clock some of the charters would have to anchor again. The winds did get to the forecasted 28 to 30 knots. Anchoring in that wind is not easy even if you know what you are doing. It was another afternoon of watching charter boats dropping anchor and drifting into other boats.

We motor-sailed from Marina Cay to The Baths, Virgin Gorda, early the next morning. We picked up a mooring ball on the first pass—woo-hoo—and snorkeled around. Visibility was not the greatest, but it was warm, and it was nice to go swimming. The piles of huge rocks along the beach were unbelievably beautiful. They looked somewhat out of place. Spanish Town, inland a mile or so, was in a valley formed by the volcanic crater. The island's caverns were molded by lava flow and the gigantic granite formations. Once at the surface, the granite was subject to weathering and erosion that removed the overburden (soil and rock), broke it into large boulders, and rounded their surfaces.

By the time we left, too many boats were again vying for too few mooring balls. Cap said they were kept up by the BVI Parks Department, but it looked like many had been neglected. (We saw lines on the bottom of the bay.) Cap said there were not nearly as many floating mooring balls as he remembered. We had a wonderful sail (albeit pinching) at 8 and 9 knots until we made the turn close to Virgin Gorda Sound, where we had to motor-sail at first, and then, just motor.

Heading up to Virgin Gorda Sound

We anchored at Leverick Bay so we could dinghy in, and I could get signed up to dive the RMS *Rhone* on Saturday with Dive BVI, an outfit that provided divemasters, instructors, and diving equipment. The RMS *Rhone* wreck was located off Salt Island, which was a bit of a motor from Virgin Gorda Sound for the dive boat, so they wanted calmer seas. They would come and pick me up at the *Lady* very early on Saturday. The Leverick Bay mooring field seemed to be better organized with more space between boats. Finally, we had an evening with no entertainment.

We motored across the small bay to a beautiful white sand beach called the Sandbox on Prickly Pear Island. It seemed to be a somewhat private beach area and a bar for the cruise ship passengers on the *Wind Spirit*, which was anchored in the bay. I wanted to go ashore to

Wind Spirit cruise ship

Lady

check it out, but I didn't want to take Little Bit, so I convinced Cap to swim in with me. The swim was wonderful. I ended up swimming round trip to the *Lady* twice because I forgot my camera the first time. We walked the beach and passed a family having a catered picnic lunch. Cap fondly called them "moneybags" because they had a 20-plus foot inflatable with a gangplank in the bow that dropped down so they could walk ashore without getting their feet wet. There were two ship's officers with stripes on their uniforms who had come ashore in their own tender,

a larger version of a dinghy. After such an enjoyable swim to the beach, the gangplank seemed a little over the top to me. Who would not want to get their feet wet in these waters? I was very glad that I was able to enjoy what must have seemed to them a simple lifestyle. Cap went up to the bar, ordered a beer (a $4.00 beer), and we grabbed a couple of beach chairs to relax while he drank it.

The Bitter End Yacht Club

We swam back to the *Lady* and motored over near Saba Rock to anchor and go to the Bitter End Yacht Club. When we were at the boat show in Annapolis the previous October, we went by the Bitter End Yacht Club booth and got some free drink coupons. I was diving the next day so I only had a few sips of one, which left Cap able to enjoy the other three. We mingled with the crowd at the beach bar and met a couple who owned a 33-foot Hunter. Putting it lightly, the Hunter was not Cap's favorite type of boat He had done a lot of research before buying the *Lady*. The owner was telling Cap he wanted to be a cruiser, but was complaining about how cheaply his boat was made. He told Cap about all the problems he was having with the boat. Cap was doing his best to listen politely and refrain from telling the guy that perhaps he should have done more research before spending his money. The guy had hired a crew to deliver the boat down to the BVI's from the Bahamas, and then he and his wife had flown down. His wife didn't really like sailing very much. Privately, Cap said to me, "Not much of a sailor, not much of a boat." I said, "Well, at least he is out there doing it." We walked down to the dinghy dock with them, and then their dinghy engine wouldn't start. I really felt for them both. I got so much enjoyment just being out on the ocean even with all the chores, maintenance, and things that went wrong, but they were not seeing it that way that night. We towed them back to their boat.

The next morning, I was up at the crack of dawn and ready with my gear for the dive boat to pick me up. My heart was pounding from excitement. On the motor out to Salt Island the divemaster gave us some of the history of the wreck. The *Rhone* was a United Kingdom Royal Mail Ship owned by the Royal Mail Steam Packet Company. It was a luxurious 310-foot-long ship with a 40-foot beam. It was considered unsinkable. There were mostly 1st class cabins.

On October 29, 1867 the RMS *Rhone* and another ship, the RMS *Conway,* were refueling on Peter Island because of a yellow fever outbreak at Saint Thomas. They were caught in the San Narciso hurricane with winds up to 130 mph. The first wave of the hurricane had both ships dragging anchor in the harbor, but both were okay. The *Rhone* had a better history of surviving bad weather, so all of the *Conway* passengers were transferred onto the RMS *Rhone*. The captains were afraid they would be run aground on Peter Island when the second wave of the hurricane hit, so they decided to make a break for a more sheltered harbor during a lull in the storm.

All of the passengers aboard the *Rhone* were tied to their bunks to keep them secure should the waves toss the ship around. At the time, this was a common maritime practice. The *Conway* motored for Road Harbour on Tortola. In trying to lift the anchor, the *Rhone* discovered that the anchor line had become wrapped around a coral head during the storm. The crew was forced to cut the 3,000-pound anchor off the anchor line because they could not get the anchor free. Without an anchor, the *Rhone* made for open water before the storm began again. The closest route to the open sea was the channel between Dead Chest Island and Black Rock Point on Salt Island. To avoid a shallow reef, the captain motored closer toward Black Rock Point. The *Rhone* was very close to open water when the eye of the storm passed, and the second wave of the hurricane began to batter her. She was thrown onto Black Rock Point. The ship had been running at full steam. When she hit the rock, and the cool sea water got onto the super-heated boilers, the explosion tore the ship in half. It sank almost immediately. Twenty-three crew members survived. The *Rhone* was initially carrying 146 passengers. There is no record of how many people were transferred from the *Conway*. A legend says one passenger survived. That passenger's cabin is now associated with the lucky porthole 50 feet under the surface. There is also a legend that the captain was thrown from the ship and never seen again.

I was excited, and I was also nervous. It was my first wreck dive. Over a hundred people lost their lives in this wreck. We would have two dives with a surface interval. The first would be on the bow of the *Rhone* up to 90 feet deep, which would be my deepest dive yet. The second dive would be on the midship/stern at around 30 to 50 feet. The divemaster buddied me up with a nice gentleman. We did our pre-dive safety checks, and then I took a giant stride into the water.

Dive boats above the RMS Rhone

Oh, that feeling again! Look at what I saw. Absolutely amazing. There were no words. There were no longer any nerves, just awe. We followed the divemaster for a little while at depth and then, as instructed in our dive briefing, my dive buddy and I moved up the wreck to 50 feet or so. We rendezvoused with the divemaster, and together we went up to 15 feet for a three-minute safety stop.

The dive boat provided water and snacks while we waited the hour to safely depressurize. That hour was also the safety interval for nitrogen off-gassing, a term I had learned in Zihuantanejo when I took my dive course. We then changed our gear onto fresh tanks, did our safety checks, and took a second giant stride for our second dive. The same feeling again. Awe. Amazement. Peace. What a beautiful world! And how lucky I felt to be under the water in that moment. The corals, the fish, the turtles. Their world.

When I got back to the *Lady*, I rinsed my gear topside in the cockpit and went down below for a hot shower. Then I got on my computer and looked at my photos, trying to identify some of the fish. Some looked good, others not as good as I would have liked. I started thinking that maybe I should get a different camera, or at least research the idea. I wanted to show people the beauty that I saw under the water. I was under the water in my mind, oblivious to the outer world, until Cap called me topside. He needed my help.

He had noticed a problem while running the generator in the past few days. He saw steam from the exhaust, but he had just changed the impeller. When we tried to make water, the generator shut down with a unit overheat error code. Cap pulled the thermostat and checked it in a pot of boiling water. Everything seemed fine so he moved on to the heat exchanger.

The heat exchanger is a two-inch pipe with tubing inside. Cold seawater runs through the pipe while the engine coolant is circulated through copper pipe. The sea water cools the coolant. This keeps the generator engine cool without being in contact with saltwater.

Cap decided to get into the repair when I got back so that I could help. He found impeller parts blocking the exchanger. While he was taking it apart, one of the brass ends came apart in three pieces. I suggested that he use his expensive dinghy patches as a gasket to help with a quick fix. I cut a few gaskets based on the size of the broken brass end. Of course, it was all his work, sweat, and expletives that finished the job. And it worked! We ran the generator and made water.

British Virgin Islands

U.S. Virgin Islands

Guadeloupe Island

Margarita Island

0   50   100 miles

Chapter 7

Saint John and Saint Thomas, United States Virgin Islands

Virgin Gorda Sound was delightful, but we needed to get back to Charlotte Amalie on Saint Thomas in the U.S. Virgin Islands to pick up my new computer, Cap's antenna, and some boat parts he had ordered. We were able to sail wing and wing—the main sail out on one side and the jenny out on the other—down the Drake Channel. It was a fast sail. We sailed around Saint John into Cruz Bay, picked up a mooring, took Little Bit into town, and checked back into the United States. Then we motor-sailed across to Saint Thomas and anchored off Red Hook for a few days. I took the bus over to Charlotte Amalie to pick up my new computer and any boat parts that had been delivered. Then I was off to the post office with postcards while Cap went to the boat

store to look for a more permanent generator repair part. He didn't find anything, so he went to a regular hardware store, where he found some plastic parts that he felt would work. They were 10 for 69¢. That would be a great deal—if they worked. We met back at the Red Hook dinghy dock and returned to the boat. I cut out two new gaskets, and Cap completed a more permanent repair on the generator heat exchanger. I started the generator up. No leaks! Cap celebrated with an early happy hour, and I went back to looking at pictures from my dive.

Red Hook anchorage with the full moon

The next morning, we motor-sailed to Little Lameshur Bay. Virgin Islands National Park had free mooring balls in the bay. With the practice I had gotten earlier, Cap and I had the teamwork down pat. First pass!

Soon after we arrived, Cap wanted to check the safety of the mooring line so we both went overboard for some snorkeling. The bay was a natural fish nursery with all sorts of juvenile fish. We looked at the bottom of the boat and decided it was time for me to get my dive gear on and clean it. It was actually quite a lot of fun in the beautiful waters. Colorful fish gathered to feed on the pieces that I scraped off as they slowly sank to the sand.

A Boobie sunning itself and a Pelican resting near where I was snorkeling

My tank had a small crease in the O-ring, and I didn't have any spares, so it was bubbling slowly. That meant that I was only able to get three-quarters of the bottom done on one tank, well, to 500 psi. I was pretty sure the crease in the O-ring happened when the dive shop in Saint Thomas filled the tank for the first time. I made a mental note that when we got back to Saint Thomas to get the tank filled, I needed to buy some spare O-rings.

We took Little Bit ashore and cleaned the bottom. We had left it in the water, pulling it behind the *Lady* with the harness since we arrived in Saint Thomas, and there were some barnacles and algae growth that we needed to clean off. Then we cleaned off the soot on the port side of *Lady*. Cap explained that the engine was a turbo with injectors that made the side get soot on her when running the engine.

There were two other sailboats in the bay. Both had gotten the "flag memo," as Cap called it. They both had very large country of origin flags flying from their stern. Cap says very few Americans have gotten the "flag memo." Both of these sailboats were British. It reminded me of the gentleman checking us into the country at Barillas Marina in El Salvador when I was sailing with Jack. The agent's pride in his El Salvador flag was memorable.

We rested the next morning because Cap was hurting from all of the chores. He took his prescription medicine, and by afternoon we were motor-sailing to Coral Bay. We made the turn into the bay and rolled up the sails. Cap had been here a few times before. I was amazed. There were 60 to 70 boats (mostly sailboats) anchored in the bay. Most of them looked abandoned, almost like they had not moved for years. Cap found a great anchoring spot relatively close to the dinghy dock. I noticed right away that there were no charter boats in the bay. There was a restaurant and bar with live music called Skinny Legs. Cap said that people drive across the island from Cruz Bay to eat at Skinny Legs because the food is so good.

Coral Bay

We went to the restaurant a little too early for dinner. I saw some shops that I wanted to check out. In the meantime, Cap found a table and ordered some drinks. By the time I came back, Cap had changed tables and struck up a conversation with a professional baseball player and an accountant who were on vacation and had made the drive from Cruz Bay. He was having a great time telling stories to this young couple, and he invited them to go sailing with us. We would pick them up in Cruz Bay and take them to Lameshur Bay for the afternoon in a couple of days.

I had at least one drink. Cap had ordered something called a bushwhacker for me. I had no idea what was in it, but it tasted like ice cream. It filled me up so much that I didn't even order the famous Skinny Legs cheeseburger.

The dinghy dock was narrow and wobbly, something I hadn't really noticed on the way in. Cap barely made it back to Little Bit. He crawled into it to wait for me. I— well, I walked on Little Bit's tubes to get farther back and get settled for the motor back to the *Lady*.

It didn't go very well. Once again, I managed to keep my shawl on at all times. Unbelievably, I didn't lose a thing overboard—not my shopping stuff, my camera, or my purse. But best of all, I did not get wet! I did get a scrape under my eye, which almost made it look like

someone hit me as I fell *into* Little Bit and right into Cap. It could have been worse if I hadn't chosen a soft spot to fall. I was so very glad that most of the chores—cleaning the bottom of the boat and buffing out the black stuff on the side—had been done earlier because I knew I wouldn't feel like doing any of them for a few days. I determined, however, to continue my sporting challenge of walking on the tubes and balancing while getting in and out of the dinghy. I enjoyed it more than the alcohol. I'd had four months on the boat, with dinghy rides too numerous to count, and I'd only had one fall. Even a mathematician would say the numbers were in my favor.

We went to Skinny Legs the next day for my cheeseburger lunch. It was very good and perhaps worth all the hype, at least once anyway. We lifted anchor and sailed down to Cruz Bay. The next day we picked up the young couple and took them for a sail up to Lameshur Bay. It wasn't really much of a sail. It was more of a motor-sail and a motor, but they enjoyed it, and we enjoyed their company. Cap was happy that they went snorkeling with me so he didn't have to.

We sailed back to Charlotte Amalie the next morning. There were at least four cruise ships in the harbor, so we stayed onboard the *Lady*. Going ashore with those crowds would not be fun. And again, the sirens wailed at night at least three or four times. I was glad that I felt safe on the *Lady* in the harbor. Both Cap and I were ready to sail farther down island. Cap wanted to get the

gearbox on the ◆outhaul rebuilt, as it had been leaking oil on the foredeck for some time. There was a facility where we could get it rebuilt on Guadalupe Island, which would be one of our next stops. Cap had also ordered an RIB and talked to the RIB dealer in Margarita, Venezuela; a new shipment would be in at the end of March.

Except for a grocery run, picking up boat parts, and waiting for the right wind and weather combination, we were ready for the next leg of our adventures! We went ashore, got our errands run, and waited. Chores always seemed to pop up when least expected. This was no exception. While we were waiting for weather, we discovered that the one-inch hose on the aft head had clogged up. Cap had already cleaned out the forward head hose so he knew what to do, and so did I. We took turns crushing the calcium deposit inside the hose. It was as hard as concrete. It took three to four hours each day for a couple of days, but we got 'er done. I then took over the entire job of clean-up. The next morning, I wanted to take all the empty boxes for recycling, as well as the trash, over to Crown Bay. Even with his medicine, Cap was not up to the 15-minute dinghy ride, so I took Little Bit over by myself. While I was there, I saw a flyer for a party, and I knew Cap would always be up for a party. It would cheer him up.

The Crown Bay Marina party had free hamburgers, hot dogs, and beer so rather than having Cap cook, we went to check it out later that day. We ran into the couple we had originally met in Virgin Gorda Sound (BVI), the ones with the Hunter 33. We didn't get the chance to talk a whole lot with them, but it seemed they had turned their experience around and were having lots of fun exploring the Virgin Islands. I was so glad to hear that.

Cap finally got a weather forecast with northeast winds that he thought would allow us to sail to our next island destination. It would be an overnight to Guadeloupe Island and Les Saintes. We put Little Bit on deck and stowed what we needed to. We would leave early the next morning with plans to island hop as we made our way south to Margarita Island, Venezuela.

Glossary

◆ *Amidships:*   The middle part of the sailboat.

◆ *Beam reach:*   Wind from the side. Between 60 and 120 degrees.

◆ *Beaufort Scale:*   A wind velocity scale. The Beaufort scale is not often used today as there are more direct methods used by meteorologists to measure wind speed and wave conditions. The Beaufort Scale is rated on a 12-point scale of 0 (calm) to 12 (hurricane). The scale was devised in 1805 by the British naval Commander—later Admiral—Sir Francis Beaufort (1774-1875). A further set of numbers (13 to 17) for very strong winds was added by the U.S. Weather Bureau in 1955.

◆ *Bow:*   The front of a boat.

◆ *Center cockpit:*   The cockpit of the sailboat is midship.

◆ *Cockpit dash:*   The dash with gauges and switches in the cockpit looks forward to the bow, much like a car's dashboard with gauges.

◆ *Companionway hatch:*   The main hatch with steps going down into the main living area of a sailboat.

◆ *Course degrees:*   The degrees on a compass that are used for navigation.

◆ *Demast:*   Break one or more of the masts on a sailing vessel in an accident or a storm.

◆ *Downwind pole system:*   A system of pole extensions to increase the amount of jenny sail when wind is coming from behind the sailboat.

◆ *Equalize the batteries:* A battery is equalized by over-charging an already fully-charged battery. The process can help take sulfate buildup off the plates inside a battery, improving performance and extending the battery's life.

◆ *Fathom:* The fathom originated as a unit of measure equal to the length from the tip of the middle finger of a man's outstretched hand to the tip of the middle finger of the other outstretched hand with arms fully extended. It is primarily used for measuring water depth. One fathom is equal to six feet.

◆ *Foredeck:* The part of the deck at the front of the sailboat.

◆ *Gin and Jigger:* Sailing with the jenny and the mizzen. Used in high-wind sailing, it helps balance the boat.

◆ *GRIB:* GRIB is a data format commonly used in meteorology to store historical and forecast weather data.

◆ *Gulf Stream:* A strong current that brings warm water from the Gulf of Mexico into the Atlantic Ocean and continues all the way up the eastern coast of the United States and Canada.

◆ *Hard Dodger:* A secure permanent frame around windows in the front of the cockpit of a sailboat.

◆ *Heeling:* The action of a sailboat leaning over in the water, pushed by the wind.

◆ *Intracoastal Waterway (ICW):* An inland waterway with some natural sections and some manmade canals that connect and make a navigable route. It provides a route along its length without the hazards of travel on the open sea.

◆ *Jenny sheet:* The lines that go from the jenny to the winch midship to control the shape of the genoa jib.

◆ *Ketch:* A two-masted sailboat with a main sail and a smaller mizzen sail.

◆ *Lee shore:* A stretch of shoreline that is to the lee side of a vessel. That means that the wind is blowing towards land, and if the anchor drags or does not hold, the boat can be blown onto shore.

◆ *Lie to:* Drop the sails and let the boat fare for itself, possibly while you go below to seek shelter.

◆ *Lifeline:* On Cap's sailboat, this was a cable that stretched from the stern to the bow of the boat under the stainless steel railings.

◆ *Mainsail:* The sail rigged on the main mast of a sailboat.

◆ *Mizzen sail:* A small triangular sail at the stern of a boat.

◆ *Out haul:* The outhaul on a sailboat is a control that connects a line and pulls the sail back toward the end of the boom.

◆ *Pinching:* Also known as close-hauled. A technique in which the sails are trimmed in tightly, acting substantially like a wing, and relying on lift to propel the craft forward on a course close to the wind. This point of sail lets a sailboat travel upwind, diagonal to the wind direction. It helps to gain ground in the direction you want to go, but loses speed, since it is less efficient.

◆ *Reverse osmosis desalination watermaker:* Ocean water is run through a series of filters. A final high-pressure pump moves the filtered water through one or more membrane housings. The wastewater, or brine, is released overboard, and the product water goes into the water tanks.

◆ *RIB:* Rigid-hull inflatable boat.

◆ *Rode:* A term that referring to anchor chain.

◆ *Scope:* The ratio of the depth of the water to the length of the chain deployed. When there is proper scope, the anchor will hold the sailboat better.

◆ *She:* Referring to a boat, an inanimate object, as "she" is a tradition retlating to the idea of a female figure, such as a mother or goddess, guiding and protecting a ship and crew.

◆ *Shrouds:* Steel cables that support the stationary objects on a sailing yacht, such as the mast. Also called standing rigging.

◆ *Skinny water:* A term commonly used to describe extremely shallow waters.

◈ *Snubber:*   A short length of non-stretchy line that is attached to the anchor chain and to a strong cleat on the sailboat, taking the load off the windlass at anchor. It is also used so the windlass does not have to take the pressure load of the chain in high wind conditions.

◈ *Specific gravity tester:*   Also known as a hydrometer. It is used to measure the specific gravity of the electrolyte solution in each cell of the battery, thus measuring a state of charge.

◈ *Stern:*   the rear of a boat.

◈ *Sugar Scoop Transom:*   Steps going down the stern of the boat to the water.

◈ *Sunbrella:*   A type of fabric along the bottom and back edge of the sail so when the sail is rolled up it is protected from UV rays.

◈ *Tacked, Tacking:*   Turning the bow of the boat through the wind so that the wind changes from one side of the boat to the other and changes the direction of the boat.

◈ *Telltails:*   Pieces of yarn or string on both sides of a sail. They help to verify that a sail is trimmed correctly. Both telltails should be streaming straight back.

◈ *VHF:*   Very high frequency radio.

◈ *Wing on wing:*   The mainsail is extended out to one side of the boat, and a pole is used to keep the jenny extended out to the other side of the boat. For downwind sails.

◈ *Winged Keel:*   Wings on either side at the tip or the bottom of the keel.

About the Author

Growing up in Washington State, the author spent her summers boating, water skiing, swimming, fishing, and crabbing at the family cabin on Port Susan Bay. As an adult, she was very content with her life, raising three children with her husband and living on a small farm in Enumclaw. She had no desire to travel. When cancer took her husband of 21 years, she struggled with what to do next. But, along with the searching and the struggles came opportunities and choices. This book grew out of her choice to reach out of her comfort zone and experience the ocean from an unusual viewpoint. Her journals and photographs have allowed her to share her sailing travel experiences with you as part of a planned series, *For the Love of Oceans*.

Lightning Source UK Ltd.
Milton Keynes UK
UKHW050315231222
414274UK00003B/41